AFTER THE WRECK

WRECK

How to Navigate the Medical Circus and Legal Loopholes

What people are saying about, *After the Wreck:*

"Having had a personal experience with insurance that was far from positive, I commend Wendy for her good work. If you want to learn the 'real deal' about our insurance and so-called healthcare industry, read this book."
— Bob Proctor, author and teacher from the movie, *The Secret*

"Wendy shares honest, straight talk about the stages of healing traumatic injuries, both physical and mental, and the journey of reclaiming your humor and joy. Read the book — be enlightened."
— Dr. S. Lane, D.C., Ph.D.

"*After The Wreck* is a humorously intense, truthful account of how the system treats you after you experience a life-altering trauma, or car wreck. If you want to hear the truth, get this book. If you don't, watch the news on TV instead."
— Keith Leon, bestselling author, publisher and book mentor

"Wendy Teague has brought her own experiences to light in, *After The Wreck.* Through courage, candor, and humor, victims and caregivers alike will find a compatriot and be encouraged to speak out to the rigmarole that is the insurance, legal, and medical aftermath to life-altering trauma."
— Bradlee Snow, author, speaker, and advocate for animals

"I admire the courage it took for Wendy Teague to write *After the Wreck.* She was brave enough to relive the past and share open heartedly so that we may learn from her experience."
— Adam Markel, CEO of Peak Potentials, speaker, author and attorney

"Bewildered, in pain, or fearful after a life-changing accident? Wendy Teague, in her book, *After The Wreck,* will walk you through the maze of doctors, insurance adjusters, lawyers and

alternative health care practitioners to get your life back on track. Her determination, courage, and wit carried her through her own life-changing 'wreck' and she can help you through yours too."
— Amy Todisco, Green Living expert, Green Lifestyle consultant and media/TV personality

"*After the Wreck* will be seen as controversial I'm sure. I admire someone who is willing to tell the painful truth from her own perspective, and somehow keep it humorous too."
— Dr. Joe Rubino, creator, LifeOptimizationCoaching.com and TheSelfEsteemBook.com

"*After the Wreck* is not just Wendy's story, it's the story of countless people who learn to relive their lives after a catastrophic injury. Knowing that Wendy made it through will inspire those following in her footsteps."
— Matthew R. Grundy, Grundy Disability Group, LLC

"As a reader, I like to go into a trance and sink into a book. And you have written a damn good book, damn good read!"
— Jo Crain, cancer survivor

AFTER THE WRECK

WRECK

How to Navigate the Medical Circus and Legal Loopholes

Wendy Teague

After The Wreck
Copyright © 2014 by Wendy Teague

Book cover design by Cathi Stevenson
bookcoverexpress.com

Cover photo by Dawn Boomsma
SurfDawn.com

Book proofed and edited by
Julie Bates & Chris Kenyon
& Peggy Zimmerman

Final proof and edit by
Elin Bullmann
TheWriteEffect.com

Interior design by Rudy Milanovich
rudy@wizardvision.com

ISBN: 978-0-9910862-0-7

Table of Contents

Acknowledgments

My deepest and most sincere, heartfelt thanks and gratitude to my Mom and my husband, Jack, for loving me through everything the roller coaster of life throws at me! I can't imagine my life without either of you.

Many thanks to my friend, Theresa Thomas, she always believed in me and this book project. She sent me the email about the "Bake Your Book" program taught by Keith Leon and Maribel Jimenez. And my book buddy, Wendy Vitalich. All of you helped me and supported me throughout my long journey from inception to completion.

Extra special thanks to my coach and mentor, Keith Leon "The Book Guy," and to his beautiful wife Maura, for being so open-hearted, loving, patient, and accepting. Thank you for supporting me, my inner voice, and my vision.

Special thanks to my friend and "photographer extraordinaire," Dawn Boomsma, for the awesome cover photo.

So many thanks to Heather Marsh for her editorial guidance and willingness to help me. To my editors, Chris Kenyon for the first cut, wordsmith Peggy Zimmerman for her polish, Julie Bates for proofing and, Elin Bullmann, for the final proof and edit. Thanks to you all for your patience and persistence.

I acknowledge the woman who ran into me, changing my trajectory and starting me on this journey, along with the doctors, lawyers and insurance companies, without whom this book would never have been written.

Thank you to all the doctors and practitioners that helped put me back together again; my lawyers for being my voice and the paralegals that kept me sane.

I thank Google and Wikipedia for their vast volumes of knowledge, making research from home a breeze. I can rest my bowling ball head whenever I need to.

Special thanks to Rudy Milanovich for the incredible layout and Cathi Stevenson for the beautiful book cover.

Much love and thanks to everyone who has loved and supported me through this journey and this book project, especially my dear friends, alphabetically, of course! Teri Bybee, Jo Crain, Sheryl King, and Tina Merritt, who were always there to pick me up when I needed an angel and a helping hand for my broken wings.

You are all amazing human beings! Much love, gratitude, and appreciation to everyone who has helped me in my process and touched my life. I would need another chapter to list all of you. My life has been enriched by knowing you!

Love, Appreciation, and Gratitude to you all! Wa-Hoooo!

Introduction

In February 2004 a woman raced out of a parking lot, turned left, and rammed straight into my car, smashing both passenger doors with enough speed and force to send my car into a tailspin. Within a few weeks, I could not stand up straight. After a few more weeks, it was obvious there were some serious problems to identify and deal with.

The seed for this book was planted years ago in my doctor's office. After months of treatment for injuries I sustained in the wreck, I blurted out "I should write a book about this! Nobody knows the whole story."

The doctor responded in delight. "That's an excellent idea. People out there really need a resource like that! You should do it!"

She thought my book would help support accident victims and their families. Most people really don't know what you go through after a wreck, unless they have been through one themselves.

After receiving her encouragement and feedback, and through much self-inquiry and using the tools I had learned over the years, I finally started to grieve and heal the life I had lost...and this book was born.

It was painful not only physically, but mentally and emotionally as well. Dealing with all the red tape was painful too. After years of fighting denial and depression, brain damage and body challenges, I accepted that it was okay not to be okay. I learned to accept my new life and to be happy with who I had become.

I wrote this book to help others weather the storm that most of us have accepted as "the system." I want to share my experience with accident survivors, trauma victims, families and caretakers. I hope this will be a guide to help others survive the system, while healing from injury. Drowning in the system can feel worse than the original injury. I want people to know they may have more options than they think.

Today, without wearing a sign around my neck, you would never know I have been in a life-altering car wreck. My picture doesn't show the years of work it took re-learning to read, write, speak, and feel joy again. Time can help you heal, but only if you put it to good use.

This is my story from my point of view and my opinions. Names have been changed but the story is true. Although not everything is presented in an actual timeline of events, I have tried to piece information together for easy reference while giving you the timeline in the chapters.

Please bear in mind that I am not a medical person. I do not have medical credentials in any way, shape, or form. Please consult your health practitioner before trying any of the techniques mentioned in this book to make sure they are right for you.

Also please bear in mind I am not a legal person, I have no legal credentials in any way, shape, or form. Please consult a legal professional for your options because different states do things differently.

"In every human being there is a special heaven, whole and unbroken."
~ Paracelsus (1493 – 1541)

"I became insane with long intervals of horrible sanity."

~ Edgar Allen Poe (1809 – 1849)

Chapter 1

I'm Fine, I'm Fine!

I heard the screams sailing unconsciously from somewhere deep inside. My white knuckles clutched the steering wheel. My car was spinning like a top. It finally came to a stop, crossing the oncoming lanes of traffic. "Slow down!" I yelled, looking out my window at the black SUV that popped over the hill. He was heading straight for me. Finally, the driver looked up, slowed down, and drove around me as if nothing had happened.

I couldn't catch my breath. There was a terrible pain in my chest, and I wondered if my ribs were broken. Still crying and shaking, I felt like a deer in the headlights. I watched traffic slow down and smoothly flow around my car. No one stopped. What's another wreck on the road?

"I am calling the police," a voice said from outside the car. She appeared out of nowhere. "Do you need an ambulance?" she asked, holding the cell phone to her ear.

Still dazed by shock and disbelief, I wondered…do I *need* an ambulance? I wasn't bleeding and I prayed nothing was broken. I figured an ambulance to the hospital would cost about $500. I slowly found the button and pushed down; I could hear the electronic purr as the window lowered.

I was dazed and disoriented. "I don't know, I don't think so. It would probably be a waste of money. I don't know," I slowly rambled through the open window.

"Can you move? Can you get out of the car?" She spoke with a hint of panic in her voice.

I turned to reach the button to release my seatbelt. The throbbing in my chest kept growing. I moved slowly, one leg at a time, grabbing my right breast in agony as I got out of the car. It felt as though my bosom had been ripped from my body. My insides felt like they had been scrambled in a blender. I assumed the pain in my chest was from the seatbelt snatching me backwards. I prayed again, more specifically, for no broken ribs.

I was still teary. The lady made sure she had my attention by looking directly into my eyes. Slowly she said, "Breathe in through your nose and out through your mouth; it will help calm you down." I taught the same technique to my clients and it was funny to hear my own teaching coming back to me from a kind stranger in such a bizarre circumstance.

I have been doing energy work for over twenty years. I retired from a previous twenty-year career in the computer world to concentrate on opening my own energy practice, "Essential Energetics," which I enjoyed for eight years. I have been a certified Resonance Repatterning® practitioner since 1997 and received my certification in the Yuen Method® in 2004. I have taught classes in Aromatherapy, Sound Healing, and Sound and Movement. I made great bath salts too.

When I changed office locations, my practice dwindled, so I returned to a "day" job to pay the bills, and my practice became part-time. I was to be transferred to a better-paying job, in the computer department as an analyst, within a few weeks. The "day" job was the reason I was on "that" road on "that" day, at "that" precise moment.

The driver who crashed into my car was there now. She must have pulled her van to the curb while my car was spinning like a top in the middle of the street.

"Are you all right?" I heard the terror in her voice and disbelief was plastered all over her face. "I am so sorry; I didn't see you." She was genuinely concerned for me.

"I don't know." I felt wobbly, like a newborn foal. My ears were ringing. I was desperately trying to regain my faculties.

"Did you hit your head?"

"I don't know."

It happened so fast...the blast of the impact and then the car spinning. I could feel the imprint of the seat belt burning across my body. My right hip was throbbing from the seat belt holder. The force of the impact was so strong that the passenger seat was smashed against the console and the console was smashed against the seat belt holder and the seat belt holder was smashed against my right hip.

The woman who called the police had run over from the car wash across the street. After she spoke with police, she asked if she could call anyone for me. "Would you call my office?" I fumbled with the number as she punched it into her cell phone.

I heard her speaking with someone. "She's pretty shaken up. I don't think she will be in to work today." When she got off the phone, she looked me over and said, "If your car is drivable, you should probably move it out of the middle of the street."

I was surprised; why would I move my car? I didn't hear any sirens. "Aren't the police coming?" I asked.

"The police aren't coming" she replied in a calm, quiet voice. "They said since no ambulance was requested, no police."

I couldn't believe it. I wondered if I had made the right choice. Everything was still shaky on the inside, but I convinced myself I was fine. I had to be fine.

I got back in my car, wincing from each move. The car started right up. I pulled out of traffic and parked against the curb behind the other woman's van. The three of us were there, in the street, next to my crunched car. The compassionate stranger told us the police said that since an ambulance wasn't requested and the cars were drivable, we were to go to the police station and do a walk-in report.

She pleaded with us both to go to the emergency room and get checked out. "You never know what injuries you may have incurred that may not show up for weeks. Please go to the hospital, both of you."

She was emphatic. *I had no idea how right she was.*

"Thank you for your help," I said looking in her kind eyes, "I really appreciate it."

"You can reach me at this number," and handed me her business card. She turned and handed a card to the other driver and then vanished as quickly as she had appeared. The other driver and I exchanged names and insurance information and then drove to the police station in Raytown.

Being back in the car made my skin crawl. I was still trembling, and traffic was heavy. When we arrived at the police station, we parked a few cars apart. When I turned off the car, I sat for a moment and tried to take a deep breath. The entire right side of my body hurt. I slowly got out of my car and looked over to see the lady who had hit me. She looked pale and pretty shaken up too. She looked like I felt.

"I think I am just starting to realize what happened," she said as she slammed her car door shut. I knew exactly where she was coming from.

I turned to her, trying to stay positive and said, "We are not broken or bloody and the cars can be fixed. It will be okay."

Once inside the station, we walked over to the front desk. We were greeted by a burly man in uniform.

We both blurted out, "We just had a wreck."

"Where'd this happen ma'am?" he asked in a gruff voice.

"On 63rd Street between the car wash and the shopping center."

When he heard the location, I could see the officer relax. "Then the wreck actually happened in Kansas City. You'll have to go to a Kansas City station to report the accident, there's nothing we can do here for you; it's out of our jurisdiction."

He sounded almost pleased that he wouldn't have to fill out paperwork. Unbelievable! The police station five minutes from the wreck can't do anything? Now we have to drive half an hour in morning traffic to another station?

We knew we needed to log an accident report with the police. I felt worse and was straining to keep it together. I took the deepest breath I could. My chest and the whole right side of my body were beginning to throb. We left the station and got back in our cars. I tried another deep breath, trying to convince myself nothing was wrong. I had to be fine.

I followed the other driver through town to the Kansas City police station. My vision would get blurry and fuzzy and then it would clear up for a minute or two. My head was reeling. I felt so conflicted. Why didn't I take the ambulance? In my next breath I would tell myself I was fine. Thankfully I had driven this road many times and I knew where we were going. False confidence helped me keep going as I kept following the other car, but I feared I would pass out.

When we arrived at the Kansas City police station, it was a tight fit to find a parking space. The other driver waited for me at her car. "I called my insurance agent on the way to the station. He will be expecting your call."

I was stunned. "I thought to myself, you just had a wreck and now you're on the phone while you're driving? Were you on the phone when you hit me?"

We entered the station and walked up to the window. The female officer behind the window was in a clean, pressed uniform. The other driver blurted out, "We just had a wreck, I am so sorry. I didn't see her."

I felt some tension release from my body. I was glad there wouldn't be a fight over whose fault it was. Somehow I trusted her to tell our story.

The officer began asking questions and taking notes. I was just standing there. I could hear her, but I had no focus. The officer asked us for our driver's licenses, promptly made copies, and politely handed them back to us. The other driver took care of most of the details.

I walked across the lobby and sat down on the hard wooden bench. I felt like I would pass out. My head was spinning so fast I thought I would vomit right there in the lobby. I got up and dragged myself back across the lobby and told the officer, "Please make sure you put down my car spun in circles. I want that documented."

"Ma'am that will be documented in your medical report," she replied in a firm tone. She continued, "Do you have any injuries?"

"My whole right side hurts," I winced, trying hard not to cry.

"Will either of you be getting medical treatment?"

"I will be seeing someone today," I said with attitude. Light headed and fearful that shock was settling in, I wanted to be home. I began wishing I had gone home and dealt with the report later. My mind raced, what will I tell Jack, my husband? My thought was interrupted by the slamming of a stapler.

"Thank you, ladies. The report will be available in a few days. I hope you feel better," she said in a dismissive tone.

The report was done. We left the station and returned to our cars to go our separate ways. I sat in my car and watched her drive away. I was mortified. All I could do was sit there and cry, sinking into a blur of emotion and confusion. Then the anger came. I still had two years of payments to make on my beautiful blue car. The anger helped me push aside the other emotions. I started my car and pulled out of the parking lot. I hope she's okay; I know she didn't hit me on purpose. I forgive her. I forgive us both.

Time would prove I would never see her again.

I cautiously drove back to the highway that would take me home. My chest was so tight I could barely breathe; my body more and more painful to move. I couldn't relax, I trusted no one on the road. Still shaking and confused, wondering why this had happened, I suddenly felt like a moving target every time another car approached. I kept waiting to wake up and find it was just a bad dream. My mind raced all the way home. What do I do next? What about our smashed car? How do I tell Jack what happened? What's going to happen to our insurance premiums? I'm fine.

Strange, it wasn't even my fault and some part of me was afraid I would get in trouble! My Jack's a great guy, I knew that's the last thing that would happen, but it still crossed my mind...I hadn't let go of one of those old trash bags of life yet. The thirty minute drive home felt like thirty days. I don't think I relaxed or took a breath once the whole way home.

I stopped just past our house. I twisted in the seat to look behind me to back the car up the driveway. Outrageous pain shot through my entire body like lightning. My chest felt like it was exploding. I turned the car off. I was finally home. I wiped my face and tried some deep breaths. After composing myself, I slowly got out of the car. I walked around to look at the other side of the car and my heart jumped. I was faced with my own mortality and at that moment I knew for sure...I could have died! The passenger side was smashed in big time. I thanked God no one was sitting there when she crashed into me.

I turned the key and opened the door. My husband, Jack, looked up, surprised to see me home from work so early. I blurted out, "I was in a wreck but I'm fine." There were a few tears but I stifled my emotions, I didn't want Jack to worry. To this day, I'm not sure which one of us I was trying to convince. But I couldn't be hurt, I didn't have time! The tape in my head kept repeating, "I'm fine, I'm fine."

I called my medical doctor's office and told the receptionist what had happened. The receptionist sounded shocked I had even called. Her tone assured me she had no time to be bothered, "We are very busy today. We don't have time to see you. If you think you are hurt you should go to the emergency room," she said rudely. Thanks for nothing I thought as I hung up the phone.

Jack called our insurance agent who did ask if I was okay. He told Jack I should go to the emergency room and get checked out. I was so confused I didn't even think to take an ice pack for my neck.

The trauma was settling in. I hurt all over.

"Most people do not listen with the intent to understand;
they listen with the intent to reply."
~ Stephen R. Covey (1932 – 2012)
"The 7 Habits of Highly Effective People"

Chapter 2

The ER

I have severe "white coat syndrome." In other words, I have so much anxiety around doctors I was hesitant to go to the ER. Western medicine can be so invasive but, after the calls, Jack and I agreed it was the best course of action. That had been the instructions from everyone, the stranger on the scene, the doctor's office, even our insurance agent. It would document receiving medical attention right after the wreck, which our insurance agent said was second only to making sure I was okay.

I saw the blood drain from Jack's face as he walked around the car and saw the crumpled doors. He glanced at me, making sure I was still standing, alive and upright. Both passenger doors were so caved in you could fit a hand through the gap between the top of the doors and the frame. Neither of the doors would open. Jack walked back around to the driver's side, looking at me with both love and pain in his eyes.

We were going to the Emergency Room. It was hard to make myself get in the car. I could feel my inner shakes showing on the outside. I was really freaked out, but I had to be fine. Jack opened the back door and helped me get in the car. It gave me the creeps looking at the inside of my car. Knowing I had been in the car when it happened was even creepier. If my car had stopped spinning suddenly because it hit a curb or another vehicle, it probably would have snapped my head off. I would be dead.

Sitting in the back seat gave me a new perspective on the damage. It made my stomach turn. Jack got in the driver's seat and started the car. Off we went to the ER. Fortunately, the closest hospital was only fifteen minutes away. I sat behind Jack feeling like a canary anticipating the proverbial cat as we drove through town. I freaked looking at all the damage; the crushed doors, the passenger's seat, and console shoved clear over to the driver's side. It was so hard to breathe, I closed my eyes. I thanked God no one had been in the passenger seat. I thanked God for Jack and I thanked God that Jack hadn't been in the passenger's seat. I thanked God I was alive.

I heard the wind whistling through the doors as Jack drove through town. They were so badly mangled; I couldn't believe the windows weren't completely blown out. My skin was crawling with shivers. When I opened my eyes, I watched every car around us; nervous, like a scared rabbit. Every car I saw made me feel the impact all over again. I was paralyzed with fear that we would be hit, so I closed my eyes the rest of the way to the ER. I knew Jack was driving and that thought made me feel safe. The pain was getting worse and harder to ignore. I could feel muscles tensing all over my body. Suddenly, oddly, sadness overtook me. My pretty blue car had been smashed with two years of payments still left on it.

I felt the car slowing down; I opened my eyes and saw "EMERGENCY" in big, bold letters. Jack pulled into the circle drive. "I'll drop you off and park the car; you go on in." I heard him, but I waited for him anyway. I appreciated the curb service so I wouldn't have to walk so far, but I was scared and didn't want to go in alone. I waited for Jack so we could go in together.

I signed in at the window, glancing at the others already waiting. I had no idea the ER visit would take so long. After about fifteen minutes, we heard a door open and the nurse called my name. We stood and followed her into a small room. She closed the door after us and took her seat behind the desk. "Now, let's get your information, shall we?" she said with a weary voice. She typed my information into her computer, obviously relieved that we had insurance. The basic medical interrogation only took about ten minutes. I mean that in the nicest way. I know they needed my history and allergies to do their job, but I was in a car wreck; who cares what year I had my appendix out?

There was a pain chart on the wall with ten faces on it. The smiley at number one had an exaggerated happy smile. The smiley at number ten had his exaggerated smile turned upside down into a frown. She asked, "At what number would you rate your pain?" Looking at the smileys confused me. I suppose it works better for small children and I was in no mood to get the kiddy treatment." About a seven." With her chart complete, she walked us back to the waiting room door. "We'll call you when the doctor is ready for you," she said as we walked into the lobby and she closed the door. I think that was code for take a seat, this will take all day. Actually that turned out to be the easiest part.

When we got to the lobby there was a man coughing all over the place. It seemed to me he was trying to get their attention more than anything else. A nurse finally came out and gave him a mask to put on. I remember thinking, "That's all I need, to catch someone's sick germs in the lobby while waiting to see a doctor." It was amazing how his cough quieted down after putting on the mask. There was a woman with an asthma attack in progress also waiting to be seen. After sitting there awhile I understood more why the man had been trying to get someone's attention. We seemed to wait forever; forgotten by the great healthcare system that would "fix" me.

After sitting another two hours, my body was stiff. I decided to make better use of my time. I called my chiropractor's office. I knew he could do more for me than the ER. I also scheduled with the massage therapist in his office. Both could see me the next day. I told the receptionist I had been sitting in the ER, to which she responded, "That's the best place to start after an auto accident; it's on your record that way. We will see you tomorrow, feel better." I hung up feeling glad I had done something constructive.

About this time an elderly couple came into the ER. The nurse looking through the window immediately buzzed the door open and another nurse was right there waiting to help them, "Mr. Girardi?"

I heard the man answer in a trembling voice, "My wife is having a heart attack." I thought it was good they had gotten in so fast, but I was sad that the nurse knew them by name. They disappeared to the other side of the door. I said a prayer for them both. My heart went out to the elderly gentleman when he came out alone and walked outside. I never knew what happened to his wife.

People came out of the big doors but no one was called back. I was impatient over and over again, and it never helped. Sitting and waiting was making my mind and body cranky. I began chatting with fellow patients waiting to be seen. Several of us decided we would be better off at home with an ice pack. Still, we waited and waited.

Finally, after five hours, my name was called from the big doors. Jack and I followed the nurse to the exam room and waited some more. At least in the exam room I could lay my throbbing body down. My brain was spinning, as if in a blender, stunned at the reality that I was in the ER, because I had been in a nasty car wreck. I was driving to work and some gal creamed me, and boom, here I am. The nurse finally reappeared and asked more questions…height, weight, you know, the kind of questions you hate to answer. It was a whole new meaning to the phrase, "Adding insult to injury." What! I'm not suffering enough so I have to admit how much I weigh?

"So how are you feeling now?" she asked.

"That wreck really hurt! The whole right side of my body hurts. I still have pain in my right breast. I think the seat belt almost ripped it off. I was spun in circles and my guts feel like scrambled eggs."

She looked me over for bruising and didn't seem too concerned when she found beauties on the underside of my right breast and on my right hip. She marked something on her chart and said, "The doctor will be in to see you shortly," and disappeared to the other side of the curtain. After a fifteen minute wait, a doctor appeared. He looked tired, overworked, and too busy to see me.

"Did you hit your head?" he said with his face buried in my chart.
"I don't know, I don't remember."

"Can you stand up?" A groan slipped out as I stood for him.

"Can you move your arms and your legs?" he said scribbling notes on the chart.

"Can you move your fingers and toes?" I moved what I could, from my head to my toes, wincing from the pain, trying to hide how scared I was.

"It doesn't appear that anything is broken. I would say you're strained and sprained all over. You're gonna hurt like hell for the next few days, but you should be alright."

"I was spun in circles and my guts feel like scrambled eggs."

"You should be fine. I will give you some prescriptions; an anti-inflammatory to keep the swelling down and another for the pain. You won't feel like doing much. Get some rest, and ice where it hurts."

"Will you write a note for work for me, please?"

"Yes, I'll get you one," he responded with his nose buried in notes.

Hmm, I thought to myself, no X-rays, no tests…this is the ER? The doctor reappeared and handed me three prescriptions and a note for work. Then he dismissed us and disappeared. I was really worried about how my guts felt and no one seemed to care but me.

I looked through the papers. The note he gave me for work had the wrong date. The office would give me an unexcused absence without the right date. So off we went through the bowels of the ER to get a new note. When we found the doctor, he seemed very perturbed with us. Too bad! It was his mistake and I needed it corrected. I wasn't leaving until I got a corrected note for work.

I was so grateful I wasn't broken and bleeding, suffering in the back of an ambulance somewhere waiting to be seen. Then again, maybe I would have gotten in faster. I'll never know. It appeared the ER won't, or can't, do anything unless you are broken, bleeding, or having a heart attack. I used to think it was the doctors, but now I think more blame goes to insurance companies for telling doctors how to practice medicine. Then again, the medical community bought into the whole insurance sales pitch "we'll make your practice and collection so much easier," and physicians let them get away with it. No wonder so many doctors prefer to retire than be told how to treat their patients.

SIX HOURS LATER...I had my paperwork in hand and was finally done with the ER. I ached all over; the pain had really settled in. It didn't help that the doctor and the nurse kept reinforcing how badly I would feel. I leaned against a pillar while Jack went to get the car.

"Do you want to come with me to the drugstore or do you want me to drop you off first?"

"Let's get them on the way home, it's faster," I said from the back seat. We stopped, Jack got the prescriptions filled, and then we headed home. Jack helped me get out of the car. I took the meds, took a hot shower, and went to bed. I felt the trauma settling deeper into my body. There was no doubt I had been smacked around. My guts still felt like scrambled eggs! I was truly blessed to be home with someone I love who loves me back. Jack was retired, and my mind relaxed a bit knowing he was at home with me.

"Troubles are often the tools by which
God fashions us for better things."
~ Henry Ward Beecher (1813 – 1887)

Chapter 3

Feeling the Wreck

When morning came, I was so stiff and sore I could barely move. I took the painkillers the ER doctor gave me and, after thirty minutes, Jack helped me sit up and then dressed me. I knew how lucky I was to be alive and I gave thanks again. If that huge SUV had hit me as my car crossed his lane, I believe I would have been road pizza!

It was less than twenty-four hours since the wreck. There was no bouncy Wendy or silly humor, no smart-ass remarks. On this day there was only pain and despair. I wanted to shut down and not feel anything. I was ready for those "few days" to be up so I would be all better again like the ER doctor said.

I was going for massage and chiropractic work, grateful they were both in the same office. I had known this chiropractor for years. I hoped he could help me. It was only a thirty minute drive to his office. It felt like thirty years.

Once again, I sat in the back seat behind Jack and looked through the top of the smashed in doors, still amazed the windows weren't blow out. Jack started the car and we headed to my appointments. I was like a nervous rabbit waiting for the fox and we hadn't even left the driveway! My fear intensified as we drove through the neighborhood and it got worse when Jack pulled onto the highway. I could hear the wind whistle between the top of the bent door frames and the roof. I looked at all the damage done to the inside of my car again. I knew it was just a car and could be fixed, but it was my car and it was sad to see it all crunched up. Thinking about the broken car was a nice distraction from thinking about my broken body, until I took a breath and my ribs exploded in pain.

Everything hurt, even with painkillers. Jack helped me out of the car and into the chiropractor's office. I was scheduled for the massage first.

"Go ahead to the third room on the right. I'll let him know you're here." Even with Jack's help, it took over ten minutes to get undressed and onto the massage table. I had never seen this massage therapist before; several friends said he was good. When he came in, he asked the usual questions about the wreck and my injuries. He explained what he would do and then he began the massage.

After I yelped a few times, Jack said, "I'll be out in the car if you need me." I knew watching me in so much pain was really hard for him. The door closed behind him and the therapist continued the massage. I could feel my torqued muscles against his hands as he tried to unwind the tight fascia that resulted from the trauma. He worked on me for so long, I could hear his next appointment complaining down the hallway.

"Excuse me," he said politely. He pulled up the sheet so I was completely covered before he left the room. He returned a few minutes later.

"I feel awful for screwing up your schedule."

"You need the work much more than she does. I got her

rescheduled; everything's fine. I am not going to worry about it; you shouldn't either." He began to work the muscles in my legs, and showed me some stretches he thought might help. Another hour later I heard, "I'm finished. How are you feeling now?"

"I feel like one giant throbbing bruise."

"Healing from a car wreck is a process, and you will get through this. Take your time getting dressed. I will meet you outside," he said, gently closing the door on his way out.

I lay on the table for a few minutes. I tried to get up, but I could barely move. Eventually I rolled onto my side and pushed myself up slowly. Every movement was a struggle; every breath a chore. I finally groaned my way four feet across the room to my clothes. I sat down and had to rest a minute. Why didn't I tell the therapist to go get Jack? I slowly pulled on my sweat pants and then my jacket. My socks were the most painful to put on. Fortunately I wear sneakers without laces so they weren't too bad. I was proud of myself for the simple act of getting dressed; something I took for granted every day. When I left the room, the massage therapist was waiting as promised.

"Let's schedule you for next week. If that needs to change after you see the doctor, he'll let me know and I will call you, okay?"

"Okay," I said, thinking to myself, this hurts too much! But, even with all the pain, I was starving and decided that was a good sign.

I went outside to find Jack sitting in the car reading one of his recording magazines. He got out and creaked opened the back door for me and helped me in. "Did it help?" he asked.

"Well, everything really hurts, I feel awful, and I cried some. I don't know if it helped or not. I'm starving, how about you?" Jack nodded in agreement. "We've got a couple of hours before the chiropractor; what do you want for lunch?" We picked a place close by that had great hamburgers. When it was time, we went back to the office for my chiropractic appointment. Jack came in with me for this one too.

Unlike the ER doctor, the first thing my chiropractor did was take X-rays. We waited while he developed them. He brought them in and put them up on the light board. "I don't see anything broken," he said inspecting the films. That was a big relief. "There are places where the spine is really torqued and twisted" he said, pointing out areas on the X-rays. "Did the ER doctor think anything was broken?"

"The ER doctor didn't really do anything. He just had me move around and didn't even take X-rays," I said with disgust.

"Well now, to be fair, ER doctors can only do what insurance companies let them do," he said in his calm, nurturing voice. "The body has so many defense systems; you won't really know what's wrong for some time. Don't rush into a settlement. It may be a couple of weeks, probably longer, before you know everything that's wrong." That made total sense; although it sounded like a lot more pain was headed my way.

The doctor helped me onto the table and proceeded to go about his work.

"I'm going to take a walk. How long do you think, Doc?" Jack said.

"I'd say about an hour, tops. Don't worry I'll take good care of her." Jack left the exam room and quietly closed the door behind him.

I told the Doc, "I have a weird swelling on one of my ribs. It really hurts sometimes." I showed him the spot.

"That's most likely flared cartilage between the rib head and the sternum (breastbone). I'll work around that area. Let me know if anything hurts too much."

He worked on me for about an hour. He's not a "bone cracker." His chiropractic style is gentle touch and technique. Gentle as he tried to be, it still hurt a lot. When he was done I was worn out, in pain, in tears, and ready to go home. After the doctor was finished, Jack was back in the room and mentioned the trip I had scheduled next week. I asked the doctor if I would be able to travel next week. He smiled reassuringly and said he thought I would be fine for traveling, but he wanted to see me when I got back. I was so relieved I had permission to go. He said he would work with me on the bill since this was an insurance accident. He told me to keep a journal of what was happening, how I was feeling and what treatments I was getting. Before I left, I made another appointment for when I returned from my trip. Jack helped me get into the car. I felt like spaghetti after all that bodywork.

"Home James," I called from the back seat, and we both chuckled.

"You try to stay relaxed on the way home." I laid back into the seat, closed my eyes, and did my best to ignore the pain and the traffic around us.

When we got home there was a message on the machine.

"Ms. Teague? This is Mike Hill with Family River Agency Insurance. Mrs. Anders called to inform us about the wreck. Please give me a call when you get in." I was feeling pretty loopy from all the meds and bodywork. I dialed the phone anyway.

"Mr. Hill, this is Wendy Teague returning your call."

"How are you feeling?"

"I'm sprained and torqued all over, we'll know more in a few weeks." I was arrogant and under the influence. I felt angry; he was wasting my time. I had been creamed in a car wreck. Did he think I would feel good?

"Have you been to a doctor?"

"I was at the ER most of the day yesterday and spent most of today with my chiropractor."

He quickly changed the subject.
"Do you remember what the driver said to you?"

"She apologized for running into me!" I said angrily. "She said she didn't see me. She even told the police that."

He quickly changed the subject again and proceeded with a list of body shops where I could take the car to get it fixed. "Don't worry Ms. Teague, Mrs. Anders is covered. We will pay to have your car fixed. We'll cover the medical bills, your lost wages, and look at pain and suffering. I hope you feel better soon."

"Yeah, so do I."I hung up the phone feeling "handled."

I wobbled hunchbacked up the stairs, and crawled onto the bed. Jack was right behind me with ice packs. He helped me strip and get under the covers. Even with ice packs and painkillers, I suffered pain throbbing through my whole body.

I wished I would wake up and it would all be just a dream. Little did I know how much pain and suffering would be involved before this was all over!

"Time and tide wait for no man."
~ Geoffrey Chaucer (1343 – 1400)

Chapter 4

The World Doesn't Stop

A week after the wreck I still had a non-stop runny nose. I was coughing and hacking up phlegm all the time. Who knew the human body could have so much snot in it all at once? The wreck shook everything loose but, because I wasn't coughing up blood, I wasn't too worried. I was, however, getting very annoyed with all the drainage. Each cough reminded me how much pain was in my whole body and my swollen rib would start throbbing with an unbearable ache. I had to assume the seatbelt was the cause of my rib injury.

I kept tissues close at hand and kept blowing and spitting. I had trouble focusing, even thinking, I told myself "it was the trauma of the accident." I kept telling myself "I wasn't hurt that badly. Things will be okay. I am fine." I had to be fine. My trip was tomorrow!

I was too sore to be excited as I packed for my trip; however, I was glad I was going. Mom was flying with me to Las Vegas. While I was in my seminar, she would visit family. We arrived in Vegas, picked up the rental car, and drove to the hotel. We had the valet park the car and Mom let him know she wouldn't need it until morning. Inside there must have been at least forty people waiting to check in. Outrageous! I stood in line and told Mom to go find a seat somewhere. She had no business standing that long; neither did I, although I didn't realize that yet.

After waiting in line for an hour and a half, I finally reached the check-in window. By then my head felt like a bowling ball and I was ready to keel over. There was a mix-up with the room. The room I reserved on the phone wasn't the room we were getting. I was outraged, but only for a moment. I was so tired and achy that I didn't care anymore. I took the room. The gift was no long walk through that noisy casino every morning on the way to class; I would be in the same wing; plus it saved me twenty bucks a night.

Finally checked in, we headed for our room all the way at the other end of the hotel. We got to the room and my head was throbbing; I just wanted to lie down. Mom was perky and excited to go out for dinner. I unpacked and suggested we order room service. After resting for a bit and unwinding from the flight, we both thought room service sounded like an excellent idea. We decided to split some chicken tenders and a salad.

My head pounded with explosive force. After five bites, I thought I would vomit. My stomach was terribly upset, and I broke out in a sweat. Mom asked if I was okay. I actually admitted I wasn't and pushed away from the table. I held my head in my hands for a minute and then headed for the bathroom. I didn't vomit, but thought I would feel better if I had. I told Mom I was going to soak in the tub and see if that would help. The room had a great bathtub! It was nice and big and held the heat well. After painkillers and soaking for thirty minutes, the pounding aches had turned to dull aches.

When I came out, Mom was relaxing on her bed watching TV. She looked me over and said, "Do you think this is from the plane flight? Maybe the trip got to you?"

"Flying never bothered me this way before the wreck," I said.

"Do you think this is from the wreck? I think this is from the wreck. Maybe we should have cancelled this trip."

"It's probably the wreck; it *has* to be the wreck," I answered, still avoiding the possibility I might be really buggered up. I had $3,000 tied up in this trip, and I couldn't get it back. The rest of the evening was nice and restful, although I ached all over.

We admired the Vegas lights from our hotel window. It's amazing how bright that city is at night. From our window, we saw a hotel with a rollercoaster on the roof! We watched it go around and around for a while; just amazed. Mom made a point of mentioning that a roller coaster ride was probably a bad idea after my wreck. I knew she was right. I wanted to ride it, but I knew it would probably create a lot more damage than I had already.

We got under the covers and watched a movie; then it was lights out and time to get some sleep. I was excited about my class, but too tired to express it. The morning would come soon enough. I saved my strength.

Our wake-up call came early. Mom was already up and getting her bag ready for her road trip, making sure her map and water bottles were within reach. I headed for the shower and got ready for class. The hot shower helped, but I still felt pretty awful.

We went down to the lobby and I hugged her goodbye. I knew she was a big girl, but I was concerned about her drive. She's my Mom. I told her to call and let me know that she got there safe. One more hug and I watched Mom walk away. A final wave and she blended into the crowd. I turned around and headed down the hall to class.

I had done energy work for twenty years and had been looking forward to this seminar for months. It was my certification class in the Yuen Method, a form of Chinese energetics. It was another technique I learned to help myself and my clients. Sadly, energy work is not mainstream yet, but it is gaining more recognition and respect as people search for answers Western medicine doesn't have. It is difficult for some to believe how amazing the human computer truly is; that the human body has the answers locked within that only need to be identified to change, and that intuition and intention alone can make drastic changes.

After registration, I was chatting and catching up with people I hadn't seen in ages. It was great to see them again, however there were headaches and strain pains throughout the week, and at times I was so scattered, I didn't know my name. I started experiencing the healer's quandary, "Why can't I fix myself?"

I worked on myself energetically at night, clearing trauma and other influences as they surfaced. Fellow students worked on me during the daytime. Time passed so quickly; suddenly it was Thursday night and we were off to our class banquet. It was a remarkable experience; so much learning and growing. I was pooped!

The next morning I was to change hotels and meet my Mom, her brother and his wife. The reservation was set up for a 10:00am check-in. Silly me, did I call the other hotel? No, I took a cab and got there about 11:00; planning on a nap and a shower before they arrived. There was no room to be had, and I was rudely informed no hotel in town had a 10:00am check-in. If I had called them before I left, I could have stayed in bed till noon at my first hotel. I went to the restaurant and cashed in on the lunch special; a great burger and fries for two bucks.

After lunch, I sat in the booth and rewrote my notes from class. After a while, I needed to get up and stretch. My neck was having trouble holding up my head. I went to the casino and played the nickel slots. I made five dollars last for an hour. I checked back in at the front desk, and there was still no room at the inn. I sat in the lobby and flipped through magazines. At least I could lean back against the couch and rest my neck. I was getting droopy, impatient, and bitchy. I went outside and sat on a bench by a waterfall. It was very relaxing, and I let my mind wander for a while. I went back inside about 2:30 and checked with the desk again. They had rooms ready…Hallelujah! Finally in the room, I took a hot shower and collapsed on the bed.

About an hour later, there was a knock on the door. The family had arrived. I was napping and not dressed for company, so I threw on a long sweater and pants to say a quick hello and give gentle hugs all around. After the drive, they were ready to rest for a while too. We made plans to meet for dinner and went to our respective quarters.

It was good to see Uncle Jim and Aunt Sally. I don't think I had seen them since Mom and I visited years ago for New Year's. We chatted through dinner and played catch-up on what everyone had been doing. After dinner, we went to the small casino in the hotel and played a few machines. They were having a good time. I was ready to lie down and told Mom I was heading for the room. I was exhausted and still denying how much damage the wreck had caused.

We met for lunch the next day and then they were off to gamble. I stayed for a bit and then told Mom, "I don't want to be rude. You guys have fun. I am going to the room to lie down." I was hoping to slip out quietly, but Jim saw me leaving and asked if I was okay.

Mom answered for me, "Jim, she's just tired. She was in a car wreck last week and she just finished a four-day intensive class, and she's tired."

I got back to the room, put on the Jackie Gleason orchestra, and snuggled under the covers. I could hear the rain pinging on the sidewalk and tapping on the air conditioner. It had cooled off. It was perfect napping weather!

About an hour later, I woke to gentle thunder as Mom came back to the room. I rolled over, half asleep, and said hi. She apologized for waking me and said she was ready for a nap too. I rolled back over and enjoyed doing nothing for the rest of the afternoon. Barely two weeks and the wreck seemed so far behind me; I ignored the bruising and the stiffness. I knew I would be okay.

We met for our last dinner together. It was a short visit and such a treat to see them again. I apologized for not being more personable. I explained I was still achy and stiff from the wreck and worn out from the seminar.

We met for a quick breakfast before our flight. Afterward, Mom checked at the front desk to make sure the shuttle was on time. We were sitting outside in the circle drive. Jim came out and chatted with us until the shuttle came. We hugged again and said our goodbyes. It was really touching. Mom and her brother Jim had been best buddies for as long as I could remember, and his wife was Mom's "sister." They were all very close and traveled together a lot. I was glad Mom could make the trip and spend time with them.

The shuttle ride didn't take long; we were the only ones going to the airport that morning. I nervously watched the traffic as the driver sailed through town. When we arrived at the airport, the line for the skycap was already a block long. We stood in line for a half hour and finally got checked in. I was more concerned for Mom than for myself. Mom lasted till we got to the desk. Once we were checked in, I saw the wheel chair parking lot and grabbed one. Mom had been standing for so long, I could see her pain. We got her in the chair and packed all our goodies in around her. We wheeled through the airport to our security gate. I learned I had no business pushing people in wheel chairs; it really zapped all my strength, but I didn't want Mom to know. Good old-fashioned denial!

The wheelchairs there have a tall steel pole on them, so you can see them, I suppose. We were waiting in line for the security checkpoint and a uniformed lady came down and said, "Follow me." We were sent to the front of the line. I have never gotten through security so fast. Once we were through the checkpoint, we were making jokes about being there so early. If we had known how fast a wheelchair gets you through security we could have slept another half hour. We got to the boarding area. No plane. There was bad weather somewhere. Planes weren't taking off and no planes were coming in. After waiting for the plane for four hours, my body was throbbing all over, even with all the stretching I had been doing.

I was starving. I went to get some food. Lines were blocks of people long so, I went to the shortest food line I could find. Mom said she wasn't hungry, but I knew she would eat if I got something for her. I grabbed some burgers, fries, and a big cola. When I got back, Mom was grateful I had gotten her something too. Typical, you get the food, and the plane shows up. We gulped down our food before boarding; I don't know why we didn't wait and eat on the plane. We boarded and flew home. When we finally arrived, four hours late, Jack was there smiling, waiting to take us home. Mom had left her car at our house and drove herself home.

I unpacked the necessities and hit the shower, then went straight to bed. I only had a few days before I had to get back to my day job. Painkillers, ice, and sleep had to make me better. I had too much to do.

Chapter 5

I Keep Getting Worse

I had a chiropractic appointment set for the end of the week. I went to work, but it was hard to focus, and sitting all day made my body throb from my head to my toes. When Friday finally came, I was ready for my appointment. Even with his gentle technique, it was still very painful as he tried to shift the twisted vertebrae. When I got home, I felt awful. After a three-hour nap, I had trouble waking up. Jack told me to go back to bed, so I did.

When Sunday came, I went to work at two in the afternoon. I was tired when I got up and the longer I sat there, the worse I felt. I asked my supervisor to let me go home early. She said "I'll try." Of course, that didn't happen. By the time I got off work at nine that evening, I thought I would die from the pain. I was afraid to drive home, but I did; I had too.

I had another appointment with the chiropractor on Monday morning. Again, it was very painful and I felt worse when he was done. I cried all the way home. I couldn't really afford it, but I called in sick to work. All I could do was cry and say I wasn't coming in. The gal who answered the phone didn't know about my wreck. When I told her what happened, she said she would take care of it and that I should stay home and take care of myself. The pain wasn't easy to explain; everything hurt! I can't think of anything that comes close; it was worse than having my tonsils out at thirty-two and worse than passing a kidney stone! It was worse than having dry sockets after having my wisdom teeth cut out!

When the pain woke me up on Tuesday morning, I called the chiropractor. The receptionist checked with the doctor who said to use ice; fifteen minutes on, then forty-five minutes off, and they would see me that afternoon. I was scheduled to work from ten-thirty in the morning until seven in the evening. I knew I would never be able to make it through the whole day and there was little chance of leaving early.

I called into work and proceeded to ice my whole backside. The numbing sensation of the ice was a welcomed relief. I went to the chiropractor at two that afternoon. When he finished, I felt even worse. I was starting to get worried and depressed. I was getting worse every week. I knew my job wouldn't wait forever, and I had bills to pay. It didn't make sense that I would feel worse every time the doctor worked on me. I had been going to Doc for years and loved his work, but it wasn't helping. I looked up and asked God, "What do I do now?"

The next day I spoke with a good friend who practices Chinese Medicine. She suggested enzymes to help rebuild the connective tissues that were injured in the wreck, and a trauma supplement to help with the raw emotions that kept surfacing. I told her I would speak to my chiropractor the next time I saw him.

That afternoon the massage therapist called to see if I could come in later in the day for my Thursday appointment. When Thursday rolled around, he called to reschedule to Saturday.

By chance, Katy, another friend who happens to be a fabulous massage therapist, called that very afternoon. I told her about the wreck and what had been going on. She offered to come by on Friday and work on me. She came to my house and worked on me for a couple of hours. I felt more relaxed than I had in weeks.

That evening, Lee, another friend who is a CranioSacral practitioner, called. I filled her in on the accident and told her that I wasn't getting better; I kept getting worse. She had some time open on the weekend and offered to work on me. I took her up on the offer and booked an appointment for CranioSacral therapy (CST) on Saturday morning. CranioSacral therapy is a hands-on approach to health care that utilizes a light touch on various key areas of the body to relieve restrictions in the dural membrane that surrounds and protects the spinal cord. Relieving these restrictions promotes the healthy flow of cerebrospinal fluid, which in turn promotes health and healing to all areas of the physical body.

The night before I saw Lee, I had a vivid dream. It was a replay of a previous experience in which Lee and I went to a hospital to support a friend who was having surgery. Lee and I were in the waiting room. The surgeon was allowing Lee in the operating room to do energy work during the surgery. While we waited, she introduced me to Nora, a friend and chiropractor she'd known for some time who happened to be there with a friend of hers, who was also in surgery. That was all I remembered about the dream, but it had all really happened some months ago.

When I woke up Saturday morning, I remembered the dream and the original experience. I called the massage therapist to cancel my appointment explaining that I'd had a massage the previous day. I didn't reschedule with him at the time. I thought I would wait and see how I felt after my appointment with Lee. I went to her place about ten-thirty. I felt very comfortable with her, and I knew my body would respond well to her work. I could feel some unwinding in my head. I even felt the depression lift a little by the time she was done.

Afterwards, we chatted, and I told Lee about my dream. She exclaimed, "That's it! You should call Nora! Nora Gallo! She's a great chiropractor and frequently works with whiplash victims. She does Atlas Orthogonal chiropractic (AO)."Lee continued to explain that Atlas Orthogonal is very specific chiropractic work. The doctor starts with X-rays to determine whether there is a misalignment of the head and neck. She assured me that Nora was very good and it might be just what I needed to straighten me out.

After my CranialSacral session with Lee I went home and got still so I could process everything. I had the dream, and Lee told me all about Dr. Nora Gallo and her work. I knew calling Nora was the "right" thing for me to do. Lee had given me so much information to take in; my brain was exhausted. I went to bed, closed my eyes and slept.

The first thing on Monday I called to make an appointment with Dr. Gallo. I explained I had been in a wreck and was referred to the doctors by Lee. The voice on the other end of the phone was kind and patient.

"We can get you in this Tuesday at 11:00am."

"I'll take it; see you tomorrow."Short and sweet; the appointment was scheduled. Now all I had to do was survive until tomorrow.

It had been a month since the wreck and I'd missed so much work already. I was waiting for the lecture. You know, when you call 1-800-I-WANT-THAT, someone needs to answer the phone and, some days, it was me. I had worked here before. It wasn't the job I wanted but, in just a couple more weeks, I would be back in the computer department where I usually worked and wanted to be.

When I got ready for work, I could barely hold my head up

in the shower. When my hair was wet, I couldn't blow it dry all at once. I had to start and stop so I could rest in between. I couldn't keep my arms up high while holding a blow dryer and a hairbrush at the same time. My arms and neck hurt so much! I wanted to blow dry my hair like I could before, but my head would pound and my body was one big humongous ache. I could barely sit down or sit up or do anything in between. My body didn't seem to be working right, but I kept telling myself I had to go to work.

I got dressed at the speed of cold molasses. When I was finally ready to go, I climbed in the car and drove the twenty-five minutes to work. I had started using a different route to avoid the spot where the wreck happened. When I got out of the car, I moved even slower. Twenty-five minutes of sitting for the drive was plenty of time for more pain and stiffness to set in.

When I got to work, the phones were buzzing away. I talked to myself in the mirror; mentally preparing for the job. "I can do this, I can do this." My body would scream back, "No you can't! No you can't!" My brain kicked in and screamed, "If you sit in that lousy, worn-out chair, you will never be able to get up. You'll freeze, stiffen up, and you won't be able to get up ever again." My body was screaming for me to listen to what it needed now, after the wreck. My brain told me I couldn't do this and yet, in the mirror, it was, "I can do this, I can do this." I had a healing practice and yet nothing I was doing was working. The inner conflict was driving me crazy.

At work, I found a station to use for the day. It was all there, the phone, the headset, the computer screen, the worn-out chair. I stood at the station for a minute, gazing. It was impossible to hold back the tears. I couldn't make myself sit down. It took a while to recuperate from sitting during the drive to work. The thought of sitting for hours, chained to a desk, made everything ache even more.

I felt like crap. I needed the paycheck. I couldn't do this. I lost it, and the tears flowed.

The shift manager came over. She knew about the accident and could tell from the looks of me that I was a nervous wreck. She spoke quietly and suggested I go downstairs and speak with Human Resources. Hannah in HR was very kind and understanding. She told me, "Go home and take care of yourself, I will have them take you off the schedule for the rest of the week. Let me know how you are doing."

"Thanks, Hannah."

"And don't forget, you will need doctor notes for the times you are gone."

"Okay."

I went home at about 1:40. I called the new chiropractor's office. My appointment wasn't until tomorrow. I thought it was worth a call to see if I could get in sooner.

The phone rang and was answered by a cheerful voice, "Chiropractic Clinic."

"Hi, this is Wendy. I had a car wreck, and I am scheduled for tomorrow. I am feeling much worse. I left work early and am calling to see if anything is available today?"

"We can get you in this evening at 8:00pm."

"I'll be there; I'll take it; see you this evening. Please don't forget to cancel the appointment I had for tomorrow," said the old hairdresser-scheduler in me.

"I've got it off the books; we'll see you tonight. Come a few minutes early to fill out paperwork."

"Thanks so much, I'll see you this evening." I hung up and told Jack I got in with the new chiropractor that evening. Then I went to bed.

When evening rolled around Jack got me out of bed, helped me dress, and drove me to the appointment. I checked in at the desk. The receptionist gave me a pound of paperwork that seemed to take hours to fill out. I was so overwhelmed by the paperwork I broke out in tears, feeling frustrated and cranky. It took thirty minutes to fill everything out. I returned it to the desk. There was too much sitting between the drive and the hard chair. When she called my name, I couldn't stand up straight, so I hobbled along behind her.

The doctor introduced herself and the first thing she did was check my blood pressure. It registered 130/90. The first thing out of Dr. Gallo's mouth was, "You're in a lot of pain, aren't you?" I could hear a gentle mix of sincere compassion and concern in her voice.

"Yes," I replied sheepishly, tears spewing forth, and there was no stopping them. She handed me some tissues and waited patiently until I was more composed.

"When you got hit, what happened?"

I took a big gulp of air between the tears and told the story again. I explained how the big white van rammed into the passenger side of my car and spun me in circles.

After hearing my story, she explained how unusual and damaging this type of wreck is. "With a rear-end whiplash, you go forward and backward; the same with a front end collision; you go backwards and forwards. The head moves too fast for the body to correct, resulting in pain and stretching of everything as the neck is going through a multi-dimensional amount of force. That type of punishment causes micro-tears in the neck and mid-back muscles and tissues, and that's whiplash. In the kind of motor accident you had, being struck from the side and spun in circles, that creates a multiple whiplash. The head keeps moving in multiple directions, even though you don't feel it. Unlike an accident when you are hit from behind, and the head only goes forward and backward."

She raised her arm with a bent elbow to represent the trunk area of the body. Then she held her forearm with her other hand to represent the seat belt. "When you are belted in, this part of your body is restricted by the seatbelt," referring to the trunk area of the body. "Your head, on the other hand, no pun intended," she grinned, "has nothing to hold it in place, so your head whips in multiple directions." Allowing her hand to go limp with the seatbelt hand holding the forearm in place, she shook her arm. Her hand flopped around in every direction. "This is what your head did while your car was spinning. You feel like you are holding your head up in one place, but it happens so fast you have no idea it's flopping all around like that. Do you understand?" It made sense. I slowly nodded my pounding head, holding back the tears I thought would never stop. I wanted my old neck back.

Dr. Gallo continued with the profile evaluation that included lots of movement and neurological tests…bend this, bend that, don't let me push down, don't let me push up, in, out. Lift this, move that. She measured and took notes every step of the way. Look this way, look that way. The one test I still remember so clearly was to tilt my head to the side, ear toward the shoulder, looking forward, and then tilt the head back. I could only tilt my head to the side about five degrees. I tried but there was no tilting backwards. Holding the position as well as I could, tears rolled down my cheeks.

"Are you feeling light-headed or dizzy?" She asked.

"Maybe a little."

"Let me know if you have problems."

"Okay."

Next, she asked me to count backward from twenty to one. "Twenty, nineteen, eighteen, seventeen…" I was astounded! There were no numbers after seventeen. My mind was totally blank. I saw the look of concern on her face. She proceeded to have me do the same test on the other side. The movement was no better, nor was the number recall counting backwards.

The many movements from the testing had my body all worked up, and the pain kept snowballing. With roughly thirty minutes of intake tests complete, she said it was time for X-rays. She took my paperwork and we walked down the hall. I hobbled along behind her, unable to keep up. Jack walked down the hall with me to the X-ray room.

I sat on the seat in the middle of the strangest looking X-ray machine I'd ever seen. She explained that the machine was very specific for taking X-rays of head and neck alignment for the chiropractic technique done at this office. The doctor positioned me, trying to be as gentle as possible and clicked her pictures. It was painful to hold the positions, but I hung in there. The worst position was bending my head way back and then leaning my chin onto the plate. It was so painful, my eyes started filling with tears again. After the click of the X-ray machine, I used my hands to pull my head into a forward position. I sure hoped these pictures would show something and provide some answers.

Tears rolled down my cheeks. The doctor smiled at me and

said, "Try to relax; the pictures are done. I'll go develop these, and we'll see what we have."

She soon returned with films in hand and put them on a light board. She was joined by her colleague, Dr. Sebastian. They began measuring with rulers and graphing lines on the films showing where my skull and first vertebrae were in relation to each other. The X-ray looked bad. With the lines drawn in, even I could tell my head was definitely not sitting on my neck correctly. The neck was severely kinked from the impact, the jerking of the seat belt, and the spinning around. Quite a combination!

The results of the earlier neurological testing along with the X-ray showing the kinked neck brought them to the conclusion that the vertebral arteries going to the brain on the right side were most likely pinched and compromising the flow of blood to the brain. That explained a lot. The next step was to do an Atlas Orthogonal adjustment.

The adjustment room had a table with a machine that looked like a drill press. Dr. Gallo explained this machine was used to adjust the Atlas, also known as C1, the first cervical vertebra that supports the base of the skull. It was named Atlas from Greek mythology referring to holding the whole world on your shoulders.

She set the AO percussion instrument based upon the X-ray line analysis. Then she had me lie down on the table on my right side. She positioned my head on a small platform, bottom arm behind me and upper arm resting on my hip. Tears were still streaming down my face, and Jack looked helpless. The machine made a clunking noise like when I got my ears pierced, yet I did not feel any pressure. After five or six taps, she had me sit up. She used a tool called an activator that looks like a fancy doorstop, and continued doing adjustments to the rest of my neck while I was sitting up. She explained what she was doing every step of the way. The alignment of the Atlas (C1) and the Axis (C2), are fundamental to how your head sits on the neck. When she was doing the neck adjustments, I felt a rush down the whole right side of my body. It felt like blood was rushing and the energy was flowing again. I felt like I was glowing in the dark, and I could even stand up straight.

"Start a journal of what's going on with you." Dr. Gallo said. I had been told that before at the other chiropractor's office. I guess it was time to do it. Before checking out, I was given plastic bags of ice and was told to use them on my neck and lower back on the ride home. I explained that I had the little freezer things that you put in coolers.

Shaking her head from the instant I started, Dr. Gallo replied, "Those don't work the same as ice. They're not as cold...use real ice. The ice will penetrate deeper and work faster."

"Okay, I will use real ice," I said begrudgingly. Then I exclaimed "It's so cold!"

"That's why you want real ice; the ice will penetrate farther and work much better."

We scheduled a follow-up appointment in two days. I was to keep up with ice on the shoulders and lower back and use heat in the middle of my back until I saw her again.

For the first time since the wreck, I felt like I could and would get better. It had been such a long month. I had no energy left. I called and cancelled the other treatment appointments that I had scheduled with other practitioners. I could feel such a change; I decided that night that Dr. Gallo was in charge!

When I returned that Friday, I told Dr. Gallo that I wasn't able to sleep because I couldn't get comfortable. I was so tired I couldn't think, and when I did think, I would get a thinking headache. She said, "That sounds like a concussion. I'm going to call and discuss this with your MD." I was falling into a pit of hopelessness. They set up more X-rays the next day at a local hospital.

It was a Saturday morning. Jack took me in for the X-rays. The technician posed me in the strangest positions. "Hold your breath," he would say and then click the picture. Every pose where my arms had to be lifted shot pain waves through my back and neck. Even my arms hurt. I was pretty teary-eyed. When the technician pulled my arms over a bar for the next picture, he seemed surprised I was crying and asked, "Does that hurt?"

"Excuse me?" I thought to myself, "Of course that hurts! Why do you think I have tears on my face?" I blurted out, "Yes, that hurts!"

Monday morning rolled around and Jack drove me to my appointment with Dr. Sebastian, who worked with Dr. Gallo. She was a chiropractor and also has a Ph.D. in sports medicine. She had me get into a gown and then explained she would be doing Myofascial Release (MFR) work to release stuck fascia. She asked if I knew what fascia was. I nodded and said, "It's that real thin tissue between the chicken breast meat and the skin."

"Yes," she said with a nod and then gave me the best explanation I'd ever heard for fascia.

"Remember when you would wear panty hose, and the hose would get a run in them?"

"Yes," I chuckled, trying to remember the last time I wore panty hose.

"That would be like a tear in the fascia. Then you put nail polish on the hose to stop the run and when it was dry, you would peel it off your leg, right? That's how the fascia works. When it gets torn, it tries to heal itself and in doing that, it gets stuck to the muscle just like the polish stuck to your leg."

"So it's kind of like a scab on the inside?" I asked.

"That's a very simple answer, but pretty much. Myofascial work is about releasing the fascia so things can move around again. It can be painful so, if it is too much for you, let me know and I will change the angle."

"Okay."

She had me lie down on my stomach and began to work on the shoulder area. When it hurt too much I would squeal and she would change the angle she was working from until the pain leveled out. If it didn't, she would move to another spot. When she worked on my shoulder, I told her I could feel it all the way down to my toes. She replied, "It's all connected." It felt like she was tugging on a body suit just under my skin. When she was done, she warned me I might be sore from the work. "Ice and heat are your two best friends right now."

Jack and I got in the car and began the drive home. My eyes kept shifting for a couple of hours. It was really a bizarre feeling. I know it was the fascia re-adjusting itself after all the work she had done. Still, it felt really bizarre.

*"The true adventurer goes forth aimless and uncalculating
to meet and greet unknown fate."*

~ O. Henry (1862—1910)

Chapter 6

Would You Prefer to Quit
or Be Fired?

About six weeks had passed since the wreck. I had spent more time at doctor appointments than I had at work. Hannah in Human Resources had been very kind and understood my situation, but I knew that couldn't go on much longer. She had her job to do, and I understood her position.

Hannah kept me off the schedule for a couple of weeks and then slowly added a few hours back in, here and there. I wanted to work, I needed to work, and I needed the paycheck! But my body would not respond to my brain, and I became a slave to my physical injuries.

The day finally came when I went to work, looked at my station, and panicked. I knew I couldn't sit there all day in pain. Typing with my arms outstretched, well, gravity always won. I knew the pattern. My left shoulder blade would start to burn, my neck would tighten, and the nerves would become pinched and angry. Sometimes my right arm would slowly go numb, while a tingling feeling started at my elbow and shot down to my ring and pinky fingers; or the neck strain would cause a blinding headache, going from my neck to my ear and across my right cheek.

My back was damaged and destabilized by the impact and the spinning. Being upright made my spine feel like a stack of unstable dominoes. After sitting for fifteen minutes, the back spasms would begin. There is a particular spot in the middle of my back that I named, "the spot where I got snapped in half." Of course, I didn't actually get snapped in half, but it sure feels like it!

I could not force myself to work that day. I told my shift supervisor I couldn't do it. Tears were flooding down my cheeks. I couldn't go near the chair. She was empathetic to my state of mind and stepped away to the phone. When she returned she told me to go speak with Hannah in Human Resources. I knew this was becoming a problem. I couldn't help it. I couldn't take the medications and work, not to mention that it's illegal to drive on these meds.

I was teary eyed in Hannah's office. She handed me a box of tissues and quietly walked to the door and closed it. She told me that when I worked, I was a great employee. However, I was not up to working and we both knew I would need more time off. My perfect record had quickly deteriorated into shambles. Hannah informed me that, because I had lost so many hours, this could result in a "resignation situation." They could no longer keep me on the schedule. I had to make the choice to quit or be fired.

She told me about a company policy of which I was unaware. If I quit, I would be able to come back to work in a few months when I was better. If I was fired due to loss of hours, I could not work there for two years. I understood the reasoning, and it still freaked me out. I told her I had no choice; I needed the job, but the wreck really changed things for me.

A few tissues later, I assured her I would forward my letter of resignation so I could come back to work when my body was ready. I drove home that day in tears. The stress was caving in on me, and I could barely breathe. My back started to spasm. I was looking forward to the burn of the ice pack when I got home.

I iced and then worked on the letter for a while. I figured if I iced more and then took a nap, I could get more comfortable and write what I needed to. I would finish the letter later. After all, I wasn't going anywhere, my job was already gone. The letter could wait another day.

Gloom hung heavy in the air when I awoke that next morning, but I finished composing my letter of resignation. It was short, sweet, and to the point. I explained why I was "encouraged" to quit my job, and I stated my case fully, in the event there was an issue concerning settlement.

I, Wendy Teague, do hereby voluntarily resign my position with this company. My last day will be March 30, 2004, for the following reasons:

I was involved in an auto accident on Feb 10,2004, while driving to work. Due to injuries suffered in the accident, I am receiving medical treatment on a daily basis. I am still unable to perform my assigned duties in the workplace. I understand that by resigning I may be allowed to return to work when this ordeal is over; and that, if I choose to be terminated for attendance, I will be unable to return to my job for two years. I understand that I must complete an Exit Interview when turning in my resignation to the Human Resource Department.

Signed, Wendy Teague

After another doctor appointment, I stopped by the office to give Hannah my letter and say goodbye. I hobbled back to the car and headed home for ice, meds, and a nap.

It was a terrible feeling to have no job, no answers, and no income to pay the bills.

It was worse to only feel semi-good when I did nothing.

Chapter 7

The First MD Visit

I called the MD's office to make an appointment and it took weeks to get one! My MD is nice and knowledgeable but, when it comes to car wrecks, there's no training for MDs. The doctor seemed allergic to me, as did almost every doctor I met along the way when I uttered the words "car wreck."

We had the car back for a few days. I thought I could handle the drive to the appointment…it was all highways with stretches at 70 miles an hour. I was afraid to drive and watched everything around me, but I got back up on the horse. When the car reached 65 miles an hour, it was very hard to handle. There was way too much play in the steering wheel and too much wobble in the tires. If I let go of the steering wheel, it could change lanes by itself. I slowed the car to less than 60 miles an hour and it was easier to control. It really freaked me out when the car started shaking like that. I thought it was going to explode. Then I thought it was the alignment. When I reached the MD's office, I sat in the car for a few minutes trying to catch my breath. The body shop didn't check out the alignment and they were told the car had spun in circles. Why wouldn't they have the sense to check that out? Why didn't we ask them to check it?

I checked in with the receptionist and was handed a pile of

paperwork to fill out, including a diagram to describe the accident. I completed the paperwork and took a seat. When my name was finally called, I was led to an exam room and given a gown. I moved at a snail's pace getting my clothes off to put on that stupid gown.

My doctor came in and took my blood pressure. I pointed out the area of my breast that had been bruised and my swollen rib. I was told that, although there might be some calcification in the breast tissue, it shouldn't be a problem down the road. "Wow, that was comforting," I thought to myself. When the doctor examined my swollen rib, she called it "costochondritis." That's fancy talk for swollen cartilage between the breastbone and the rib head. I explained how much it hurt when I used my arms or hands to push down, push together, or try to screw off a lid.

I let the doctor know I was seeing an Atlas Orthogonal chiropractor. She had never heard of it. That was no surprise; neither had I until recently. I bragged that I could stand up straight after my first visit and I was using a lot of ice too. I also brought up the chiropractor's theory that the vertebra and the skull had been so far off kilter, it may have been putting pressure on the vertebral arteries and impeding some of the blood supply to my brain.

I got the big eye roll on that one; the standard response to that theory from most doctors. I don't understand why. I saw the X-rays and I could see the misalignment that could compromise the vertebral artery. It still amazes me how some doctors seem to ignore what they don't understand.

I told her I was having bad headaches and thought I had a concussion.

The doctor immediately asked, "Did you hit your head?"

"I don't remember," I said, struggling to remember what happened.

"When the car stopped, did it stop because the car came to a stop by itself, or did the car stop because it hit something?"

"No, the car stopped on its own after spinning."

"Well if you didn't hit your head, you wouldn't have a concussion."

I was pretty sure I had a concussion; the outrageous headaches, the thinking headaches, and there was constantly pain in my head and neck. The doctor thought I would be fine and gave me a mild muscle relaxer to help with pain and sleep and wanted me to take a prescription anti-inflammatory for the swollen cartilage on my rib. Knowing its reputation, I objected to the anti-inflammatory, but she convinced me to try a five-day sample.

The doctor finished her notes and checked the clock. I knew my time was up. "If the chiropractic is working, keep doing it," and then after some hesitation she said, "If you're not feeling better, make another appointment."

I was concerned about her lack of concern. I had been in a serious car wreck! I was spun around in circles and my guts still felt like scrambled eggs. Things were wrong; my body wasn't working right. An MD tells me to keep seeing a chiropractor? That had never happened before. I think the doctor was glad I was seeing someone else, so she was off the hook. I was glad I was seeing someone else too. After working with Dr. Gallo and Dr. Sebastian, I was convinced they knew a whole lot more about car wreck injuries than most MDs ever would.

I left the doctor's office and headed home, keeping the car just under sixty miles an hour. I felt abandoned by my doctor. I felt betrayed and lost without any real answers. I was looking forward to the sting of an ice pack when I got home. I was exhausted and could barely hold my head up. I kept thinking, "That's Western Medicine for you." I thought it was interesting the only people concerned enough to get X-rays were my chiropractors.

When I got home, I was so happy to see Jack! I was trembling from the drive home and needed a good hug. Sadly, my body could not withstand the pressure. Jack had an ice pack ready and asked what the doctor said. I told him "not much." I took the anti-inflammatory for 5 days, with no apparent difference in the size or the pain in my swollen rib. Months later, my skepticism was validated when that particular drug was yanked off the market. I'm sure glad it didn't kill me.

I told Jack about the car and how it was acting. Either something was still bent or the alignment was way off. He was furious!

When the phone rang that night, Jack answered. "How could you release a car in that condition," I heard him yell into the phone. "My wife was driving that car today and nearly scared her to death. You're damn right I'm bringing it back." I had rarely seen Jack that mad. He even slammed down the phone.

"Who was that?" I asked.

"That was the body shop checking to see how the car was running. I'll take it back in the morning. I don't understand why they didn't check the alignment before they released the car. That's ridiculous!"

I felt sorry for the person on the other end of the phone. They picked a bad time to call and Jack really read them the riot act! I called the insurance company and we picked up another rental and dropped my car off at the auto body shop. Jack was still really mad. The man at the shop apologized profusely. I could tell by the look in the girl's eyes at the counter she was the one he had yelled at. I sat there paralyzed by the confrontation. We were offered the option to wait, but Jack told him we had already picked up a rental car and to call when it was done. Three days later, we got the call that the car was ready. I had no doubt they had gone over it with a fine-tooth comb. We picked up the car and drove on the highway to check it out before returning the rental. They fixed it.

"Sometimes even to live is an act of courage."
~ Seneca (ca. 4 BC — AD 65)

Chapter 8

Thinking Headaches

It has been well over a month since the wreck, and I still walk a thin line between agony and prayer. The few days I did work were awful! I couldn't focus. Looking at email gave me a headache. When I thought, I got a headache and when I thought really hard, I got a *really* bad headache. I *must* have a concussion; what else could this possibly be? If I don't have a concussion, why does my head throb and pound? Do I have migraines now? Once the headaches start, there's just no stopping them.

I can't read. I can't do math. No concussion my butt! Thinking gives me brutal headaches. I stutter playing word association until the word that comes out of my mouth is the word my brain is trying to express. It's like my brain is always playing Scrabble®. Since I make up terms as I go, I would diagnosis Scrabble® mouth! I am exhausted from the pain and all the changes that have taken place as a result of the wreck. Small, everyday chores are total challenges. Did I actually tell the MD that? I could barely remember the appointment.

Some mornings I wake up so stiff, I use my heating pad like a giant iron. I gently rub the warm heating pad over my chest and abdomen and then up and down my arms and legs. It warms and loosens my muscles so I can move.

I was chatting with a friend telling her about what had happened. "I am convinced it's a concussion. I don't know why the MD isn't convinced."

"Shaken Baby Syndrome!" she exclaimed. "No really, think about it. Your car was hit so hard that it spun in circles, right? You were, simply, all shook up! Now wouldn't that have the same force, probably more, than a grown-up shaking a baby?"

With all the problems I was having, it was an explanation that made sense. Over a month and the mucous is still draining from my body. Years later a friend taught me that much mucous was a sign of inflammation. The mucous was coating and cushioning, trying to protect the body from further injury.

Things that used to be so enjoyable, like watching TV or reading a book, made my head hurt. I still haven't found a comfortable reading position. It's so difficult to hold up a book, and I don't understand a word; it's like a foreign language. The headache becomes unbearable and none of the words make any sense. I just see gibberish.

Sometimes I have to close my eyes so I can really hear the TV... and now when I see a wreck on TV, I rewind it and watch it in slow motion backwards and forwards, over and over again. I have no idea what I'm looking for or hoping to figure out. It's a new obsession born from the wreck.

Math was another problem entirely! That fall, I spent the day with friends at their garage sale. A little girl came up to me with two items. One of the items was marked five cents and the other was marked twenty-five cents. I knew the symbols and numbers; I didn't know what they meant. I didn't know how much it was; I couldn't add the two together. I handed them to my buddy and said, "Here, how much is this?"

She glanced at me with concern, then with a smile told the child "thirty cents." The child happily handed the coins to her and skipped away. "That wreck really messed you up, didn't it? I had no idea it was so bad. What's it been, six months?"

I proceeded to count on my fingers, "February, March, April, May, June, July, August, and now its September, so that's eight months."

"Wow!" she said with disbelief. "I really didn't know it was that bad. You will get better, right?"

"Time will tell. At the moment I can't even do garage-sale math."

I tried to balance my checkbook; it's just a mass of numbers. I can't even use my adding machine correctly and that's really depressing. I used to be great at ten key, having used it for decades. Funny, I would never have expected to hear myself say I missed knowing how to do math. I was never a math hound, but I was great at calculators and computers. Now I can't even add five cents and twenty-five cents together; that was quite a reality check.

When I wrote, my letters would flip. For example, "q" would become "b" and "g'" would become "p" and there were others. When spelling, I could see the word in my mind but I couldn't get it to come out through the pen. I also found it very difficult to stay inside the lines, even on wide-lined paper. The words I see in my head come out on the paper as strange words.

One weekend at Mom's we were watching a movie. "Who is that guy?" I asked her.

"James Mason," she replied.

"That's not James Mason."

"Wendy, that is James Mason."

"No, it's not."

She gently repeated herself "Wendy that is James Mason."

"I will have to trust you because the person I see in my head as James Mason is not that person on TV." I began to repeat his name over and over to myself while looking at his face, as if I were reloading the data in my brain. I did a lot of that "reloading data" thing. It's like the little synapses in my brain were knocked off about three hairs, so all the indexing was out of whack.

Dr. Gallo banned me from gardening. She said, "just use containers; you can't garden the way you used to garden. I have been using containers and pots for years. They work out really well. You don't have to till soil and you can move them around whenever you want to, although you'd better ask Jack to move them for you. That would be a better idea for you and your back." Another joy of life no longer on my "I can do it" list.

It's embarrassing to admit, but it took me two weeks to come up with a support for bean plants, but I didn't give up! Every day I would think for about thirty minutes and draw picture after picture until I finally thought I had it all figured out. When I went into the yard to execute my plan, nothing seemed right. It took me three days just to put string on sticks to hold up the bean plants. It's a simple, logical, and straightforward project. I've been putting up bean poles for decades. All I wanted to do was plant some green beans and I felt totally out of my comfort zone.

My mechanical, logical brain didn't seem to function anymore, as if all the logic in my brain flew out through my ear when I got hit. My problem-solving skills disappeared. I missed my old brain.

Such little things could bring on a monstrous headache. After a while, I knew which headache was which. If the pain was in the lower part of my head, on the backside, I knew I needed ice. If the pain started at the base of my neck with little daggers working their way up to my ear, I was in trouble. The trigeminal nerve was pinched, and soon overwhelming pain would invade my face. The trigeminal nerve branches out to the eye area, the cheek area, and the jaw. It got so bad some days that I'd look up and say, "If you're gonna take me, take me now." The doctor at the ER said I would be in a lot of pain for four days; he forgot to mention the weeks, months, and years of pain still to come.

I think my friend was right about the Shaken Baby Syndrome idea. My car was hit really hard and spun like a top. For a grown-up, that could equate to Shaken Baby Syndrome. Don't you think so? After all, my poor brain was bouncing around inside my skull like a ping pong ball. In a car, there is nothing to hold your head in place or protect your head.

Even in football, when a player is hit while wearing a helmet, the brain is in there bouncing around. Football players get concussions all the time just from the jolt of the impact. They don't need to hit their head. No matter what helmet they come up with, there is still no protection between the brain and the skull. Until the brain can be stabilized inside the skull, people will continue to have concussions. Had I been injured while playing sports, I can only imagine the treatment would have been different. I have seen football players who had been out with concussions come back to the game too early. I could feel it. I could see it. The way they moved; the way they looked. They just weren't all there. That was how I felt!

Now when a football player has a concussion, they take it seriously. I have read that now, if you have a concussion, they recommend that the brain rest…no input, no TV, no computer. It's the only way the brain can truly rest. Today, concussions are a widely-discussed ailment; they're the subject of TV specials and magazine articles. But ten years ago when I had my accident, no one told me to rest my brain! If I had been told that, then maybe I wouldn't have so many brain problems today.

If my brain had rested and had time to recuperate, the way muscles and tendons do, who's to say what my condition today would be? Can't let the "what if's" drive me nutty. What happened, happened. There's no point in would-a-been's or could-a-been's because it's not what happened, so what does it matter? How is it useful? Forgive, let go, and be grateful you're alive. This is life now, and now is all we have. There are no dress rehearsals.

Dr. Gallo knew it from day one. Plus, Dr. Gallo had taken X-rays that showed how my neck was kinked and twisted. She said it was the worst case she had ever seen. Looking at the X-rays was really bizarre. I couldn't really see what she was seeing. In AO chiropractic, they focus first on how the head is sitting on the neck. They took the X-rays and put them up on the light board, took out rulers, and drew a grid on the X-rays. Once that was done I could actually see that my block was almost knocked off, so to speak. It was freaky to think that if my head continued to be jarred, or my car had been stopped by another car, I would most likely be dead. Stay grateful for what you still have.

Later on in the fall, my physical therapist told me he was certain I had a concussion. He said, "Concussion and whiplash usually go hand in hand. When you don't hit your head it's referred to as "contrecoup" which basically means you didn't take a direct hit to the head but your brain is still bouncing around in your skull." He explained it in the same way Dr. Gallo had, making motions with his hand showing me how my head was flung around in every direction. "And when that was going on, your brain kept bouncing off of different places in your skull. I have no doubt that you had a concussion." Finally, some traditional validation, I was not crazy. I had a concussion.

"Healing is a matter of time, but sometimes also a matter of opportunity."
~Hippocrates (c. 460 BC – c. 370 BC)

Chapter 9

Releasing Trauma with Body Work

I've been studying, using, experimenting with, and teaching energetic healing techniques for decades. It was called "New Age" for awhile, even though the techniques were thousands of years old. Now the mainstream refers to it as "Complementary" or "Alternative Medicine." That never made sense to me. Complementary sounds just like complimentary which means free and alternative means substitute, neither of which are necessarily true.

I am intimately aware of how pain and trauma can change your personality. Most days I spent exhausted from being exhausted, of being exhausted. I was filled with anger and frustration. I withdrew from the world, my friends, and my family. I was not yet back to a place where I could feel the subtleties of energy work, which was frustrating.

Ironically, I had been asking the universe for a class in anatomy and physiology. I did not expect to be studying on my own body. Now it had been about three months since the wreck. I'd been seeing Dr. Gallo for about six weeks. She often said, "I wish you would have been in here the day after the motor vehicle accident. The muscle memory had a month to set in before we ever saw you. This will take some time." I cried frequently during my appointments and was always treated with nurturing earth energy. During one breakdown, Dr. Gallo handed me a box of tissues and a bag of oyster crackers. "Now these are the real oyster crackers; we ordered them in from New England. I want you to take these home with you, use the tissues, eat the crackers, and don't forget to ice." I was still crying but it made me feel better to hear that she cared.

Working with both doctors was a hoot. I still work with both doctors. Dr. Gallo told me that if it ever hurt, I should squeal out, "Oh, stop that Dr. Sebastian." On the other hand, when Dr. Sebastian was working on me and it hurt, I was to squeal out, "Oh, stop that Dr. Gallo." I have to admit it was fun and it did help me to shift my focus away from the pain. The two complement each other so well; they make an incredible healing team. After working with them two or three times a week, they felt like family. Jack would drive me to my appointments and read his magazine in the car. They knew he really did exist because every once and awhile he would come in and use the bathroom. I knew why he preferred to stay outside. My whole body was so tender, sometimes during Myofascial Release work I would squeal out; much better than holding it inside!

Most of the time after receiving body work, I could feel my body shifting. Some days I would be exhausted; other days I had spasms; still other days I would crave red meat. I was telling Lee about that and she said not to worry.

"Your body is probably craving beef for the specific amino acids beef has to help your muscles heal. I wouldn't worry about it. When your body has had enough, you will stop craving it so often."

One time Dr. Sebastian was working on my right shoulder

doing Myofascial Release. Something released and I felt a ripple effect, like a slinky under my skin, spiraling and unraveling from my shoulder down my wrist and through my hand. It was amazing. Many times after having Myofascial Release my eyes would move around for hours. It is true, it is all connected. She worked on my back and my eyes moved around. Of course, you move the fascia in one place and it affects the rest. It's like tugging on one-piece, fitted pajamas. She would pull the shoulder and I would feel it move in my leg. A pull on the foot and I would feel it all the way up to my neck. Fascia is everywhere…it's everywhere! It's *all* connected!

In fact, it was Dr. Sebastian and Myofascial Release that inspired me to come up with my slap scale. When I was at the ER, the nurse used a pain scale from one to ten ranging from really happy faces to really sad faces for me to rate my pain. After having Myofascial Release work done a few times, I came up with my slap scale of one to ten for how many times I wanted to slap her. When Dr. Sebastian hit a spot that was a six-slap or above, I would tell her what number my pain was. Over the years she had learned how to position herself strategically so there was no way I could slap her. It was a way to have fun during our sessions and also would let her know my pain level. As painful as Myofascial Release can be, I felt better within a day or two, most every time.

After months, my body finally started to stabilize. I would feel the benefits of a chiropractic adjustment longer than just a few days. My back wasn't in spasm every day. Several times a week, the outer tendons at the little round ankle bone(outer base of the fibula) would tighten so much, it would force my feet out and up like I was trying to walk on the inside of my ankles. Truly painful! After years of experimenting, I know to stand up and lean against the wall, slowly putting pressure on one foot at a time to flatten them against the floor. Once they can hold their regular position when I take a step, I walk around slowly until the tendon releases. Some days it takes half an hour, some days only five minutes. Gratefully, these attacks have become infrequent.

I knew how much the adjustments and body work were helping. Jack could see a difference too. It felt different each time I had work done. Different work yields different results. Through trial and error, pain and suffering, I learned that the order in which I received treatments made all the difference in the world. At first Dr. Gallo was skeptical about me having so much work done within such a short period of time, so I explained how it worked for me. I felt that seeing her first for an adjustment helped assist Dr. Sebastian with Myofascial Release because, as I was now aligned, it would help the muscles adjust and realign to generate new muscle memory; then on to the work with Lee for CranioSacral therapy.

Lee's work is always wonderful. She brings years of experience in energy work to the table, literally. She is trained in many techniques, such as Attunement and Reiki (both energetic healing methods), and blends them beautifully into her CranioSacral work, when appropriate.

When I first saw Lee after the wreck, I told her, "I can't feel my energy moving. I could always feel my energy move before, but not since the wreck. What if my ability with subtle energy never comes back?" I could feel tears welling up.

Lee softly said, "Take a nice deep breath...stop the worry...just relax...it will come back...just give it time." After she worked on me, I knew there had been an emotional release, as well as physical. Her work could make me cry, pouring out emotions instead of crying out in pain. I always felt so much calmer. After the physical endurance of adjustments and Myofascial Release, having that subtle CranioSacral work would help realign my energy.

"CranioSacral is mainstream, isn't it?" I asked Lee.

"Not even close, honey."

"How can people not know about this work?" I said with a confused stutter.

Lee shrugged her shoulders and said, "We know it works. It takes time to learn, and mainstream medicine doesn't want to deal with it, so there you have it."

I knew she was right. I was certified in Resonance Repatterning in 1997, (formerly known as Holographic Repatterning) the year I started my private energy practice. I was still explaining "resonance" and "coherence" to people who had never heard the words before. I think it is amazing how the word resonance seems to be used everywhere now. I remember the first time I heard the word on TV. The news guy said, "I think that resonates with the whole country." I was stunned that, after explaining resonance to people for years, the word resonance had become a buzzword. I like to think that Resonance Repatterning, and all of the practitioners using it, played a role in bringing the word resonance into the mass consciousness.

I lived in a different culture of wellness than mainstream medicine. Don't get me wrong, there are things mainstream medicine does well, but my own experience after the wreck made me feel as if I were parted out just like a wrecked car. There's one doctor for this and another doctor for that, and there's a bill from another doctor you didn't even know existed. Tell me, have you ever actually seen a Radiologist? How about a Pathologist? I see the bills, but I've never seen a Radiologist read my films or a Pathologist look at my blood work.

For decades I have understood the body is energy. Everything is energy. How many times had I explained that to clients? It always made sense to me. Shift the energy and you shift the body. Whether you are working with physical, emotional, mental, psychological, or spiritual energy, you are working with intention to create a positive shift in the energy. That shift creates a ripple effect that spreads out to affect the whole person. That person changes and sends out different ripples to others. When you throw a rock into a pond, you create ripples in the water. The water will eventually calm down and look the same. However the rock is now under the water and has changed the pond forever.

Does someone else's bad mood make you have a bad day? When someone across the room is laughing, do you start to giggle? When you feel fine and there's a foot of snow outside; when you see a commercial about sore throats on TV; does your throat feel sore all of a sudden? These are examples of subtle energy shifts.

The chiropractors told me to hold off on massage for a few months to give the tissues healing time. When I was allowed to have massage, I called Katy for help. She is fabulous! She knows so many types of massage and energy work. I remember one day she was staring at me, studying my neck.

"Where's your SCM, honey?" she said. "I can't see it." The SCM or Sternocleidomastoid is a paired muscle in the neck that splits and inserts behind the ears. When you turn your head all the way to either side, you can feel the SCM muscle at the base of your neck headed toward your ear. You can also see it in the mirror when you turn your head to the side. It's an important muscle for neck movement. I looked in the mirror and she was right, there was no SCM showing on either side.

When I was on the table she began working with my neck and upper back loosening the muscles. She warned me, "This is probably going to hurt. I'm going to pop that SCM loose."

"Okay, let's go for it," I said. She wasn't kidding! I let out a yelp!

"Now move your head around and see how that feels." The pain didn't last long at all. I was amazed at the difference in my neck. I rolled my head from side to side. I had to get up and look in the mirror. There it was every time I turned my head. I was stunned I had not noticed that before. Dr. Gallo and Dr. Sebastian agreed it was time I worked massage into my body maintenance routine. Katy could also help with the fascia issues.

"Life is made up of sobs, sniffles, and smiles,
with sniffles predominating."
~O. Henry (1862 – 1910)

Chapter 10

Some Days,
A Head IS Just a Bowling Ball

This is my explanation, opinion, and observation of the medical enigma known as whiplash. I have come to learn that some days your head IS a bowling ball. Whiplash changes everything. Explaining whiplash and the effect that comes with it is difficult; I don't even think that most doctors understand it. During all that movement of being thrown around, the neck becomes full of micro-tears in the tissues; quite possibly in the brain as well, since your brain is like a ping pong ball bouncing around inside the skull.

The average weight of an adult head is approximately twelve to fifteen pounds, just like a bowling ball. When the head moves, the neck follows. It has no choice. The head and neck are thrown around and bent in every direction while you are spinning in a car, totally against Mother Nature's intended natural mobility. I had no control of the car or myself. I went straight to pure survival instinct mode and hung on tight. Everything happened so fast; I have no conscious memory of what my head actually did during the wreck. I remember leaning forward into the steering wheel while looking back at the other car, trying to get out of the way. When it smashed into the side of my car, I was jolted to the left, my shoulder belt yanking me backwards, and the lap belt yanked down tightly across my hips, all at the same time, while the car was spinning. That's a lot of directions for the head to be thrown in all at once.

It's amazing how often we take our bodies for granted, especially the neck, which is the bridge between brain and body. Simple movements, like looking up at a clear blue sky or admiring the night stars, are not really possible with whiplash. A great tip Dr. Sebastian gave me was, "If you want to look at the stars, lie down outside on a blanket so you are looking ahead instead of up."

When looking up, my neck locks, and I have to grab my hair or the back of my head and pull my head back over my neck. When looking down, like reading, I have to put my fist under my chin and push my head back up.

When Jack is driving and we are about to cross a set of train tracks, I brace my neck by putting the heel of my hands under my jaw and wrapping my fingers around the back of my head. I pull up straight a little bit for easier shock absorption when we go over the tracks. Others may not even notice the bumps, but those tracks are still hard for me, even though Jack goes over them slowly for me.

A song came to mind, "Put my head on my shoulders…" Yeah, for real man! I was singing it! I was learning to have fun with it; it was helping to lighten the load. Laughter is an amazing antidote, unless it causes pain. It would be years until I could enjoy a great rib spreading laughter. Those intercostal muscles that run between the ribs can be a real bear!

What about something simple like washing dishes? Arms extended straight out in front of you, the weight of the plate, and the scrubbing motion engages the arms. The arms engage the neck, and then the head and shoulders join the party. The weight pulls my arms, which pulls on the neck, which pulls on the head and shoulders. Soon my left shoulder starts to burn and the right hip starts to feel weak. It's past time for a break. It IS all connected.

I miss being able to get out of the shower and shake my head like a dog to get the water out of my hair. Speaking of my hair, I've kept it short since the wreck. When my hair got long, my neck was too weak to support my wet head! Even with my short hair, I can't hold my head and arms up at the same time long enough to blow my hair dry. Keeping my arms up with the blow dryer in one hand and brush in the other for more than a few minutes will usually start back spasms. My neck gets so weak it feels like my head will fall off and roll across the floor.

It's interesting to me that the arms are so connected to the neck. Picking up a gallon of milk can really tweak my neck. I have learned that picking something up and jerking it up affects the neck completely differently.

My neck is now completely different. It's amazing how many parts the neck has: the vertebrae, nerves, muscles, circulatory, lymphatic. All the strength is zapped. Like untying a splice in a rope and then trying to splice it again so it all looks the same. This is tricky business. The micro-tears in all the muscles probably look like ruffled edges instead of the nice smooth muscle that was there three minutes ago.

When I have an appointment with Dr. Gallo and I ask her to put my head back on, I am being quite literal. The thoracic area (base of the neck to waist) of my back feels like a set of dominoes. When I'm sitting, it feels that any second one domino will pop out of the pile, and I will collapse. Imagine a bowling ball resting gently on a stack of cooked pasta. Not a solid foundation for the bowling ball, is it? Now... picture that bowling ball as your head, sitting on that pasta that used to be your neck. Doesn't sound good, does it? Whiplash creates tons of micro-tears you can't see, but you can definitely feel the impact! Since science has no way to take pictures of them or measure them, the sin of soft-tissue damage rears its ugly head. Say "soft-tissue injury" and insurance companies laugh and rarely pay enough to cover the bills.

Imagine holding buckets of water at shoulder height; arms straight out to your sides. Imagine those heavy buckets in your hands; feel the pain of the weight exhausting your shoulder muscles, tugging at your neck, constricting your back. Soon you feel your shoulders slowly giving out as the buckets begin to feel like they weigh tons instead of pounds. Your arms and shoulders can no longer hold up the buckets. The pain becomes excruciating and soon your body collapses. Now... imagine that painful exhaustion is your neck. How does one hold up their head? Some days I can stay upright for half an hour if I'm not too rambunctious, and then I have to lie down a few hours and take the weight off my neck and back.

Some days my head is just a bowling ball, and on a really bad day, it's a gutter ball!

"Experience is the best teacher but the tuition is high."

~ Norwegian Proverb

Chapter 11

The Road Trip

Once again, I was at the chiropractor's office for tissue work, about four months after the wreck. Once again, I threatened to write a book about the wreck and all that comes afterward. Dr. Sebastian said, "That's a great idea; we could use a great book to support patients and their families, and people who are in that situation. People don't know what you have to go through after a motor vehicle accident, especially one like yours; it was a bizarre one. Make sure you put in the effect of trauma on personality in your book." She was emphatic about that.

I knew exactly what she was talking about. That feeling of overwhelm that could paralyze me, and the impact of anxiety attacks and panic attacks. Sometimes it comes over me slowly and, sometimes, hits me like a tidal wave. My fears rise up. Anything or anyone on the road makes me anxious. White vehicles, big vehicles, and semi-trailers, make me super anxious. Some days the panic is so overwhelming, I have to pull off the road until I can breathe again.

The panic was rising again. I was afraid of her reaction, but I had to tell her. "Dr. Sebastian, I have a road trip to Arkansas coming up. I have two more appointments scheduled before my trip. The second one is the day before I leave. Think I can make it?"

"Well, it sounds like you're going to find out," she said, looking at me over her glasses.

"Faith is getting her Master's degree and I have to be there. She's my 'adopted' niece. I was there when she was baptized and when she graduated from high school; I was there for her wedding and I want to be there when she graduates with her Master's degree."

"You still have a lot of physical issues we are working with."

"Jack and I talked it over. Instead of driving the full eight hours in one day, I'll stop at a hotel and just drive 4 hours a day. That would give me plenty of time to stop and stretch when I needed to, and time to lie down and ice." She was right; I was still having a lot of problems. I was so frustrated that my body wasn't completely healed, but I just had to go.

"Make sure you ice before and after you drive. Stop when you need to and stretch for at least 15 minutes. Come see me when you get back."

After my session, she walked with me to the reception area. She looked at me and said, "Now you make sure you put in the effect of trauma on the personality in your book. You know what it does, and you're living it. People need to know. That's the part nobody addresses and people need to be told about it." I made my follow-up appointment and, with a hug and ice bag on each shoulder, I headed home.

I knew the effects she was talking about; the confusion and depression that creeps in; the panic attacks; having no control over your emotions. Isolating myself so as not to burden anyone; cutting yourself off from life when you really need to reconnect to it. You do need to know things after a wreck that no one can share with you unless they have lived it too. Medical options, legal options, every state is different so do your homework.

I was slow moving the morning I left. I was excited to see everyone, but the drive felt daunting. I packed three small bags, one for each leg of the trip. That would be less weight to carry, and I could keep track of things easier.

"Do you have your ice bags and your heating pad in there somewhere?" Jack said as he looked at my bags.

"Yes, they're right on top. Would you put one of those coolers in front?"

"No problem, you've got two pops and water in this one with lots of ice. The cooler in the back has the same. They're small enough that you can leave them in the car and lean them over to drain the water. You take it easy, okay? You get out and stretch a lot, okay?"

"I'll be fine, I have to be." I knew he was concerned and so was I.

"Call me when you stop, okay honey?"

"Absolutely, stopping halfway should help me feel better for the graduation. I promise, I will ice and stretch."

After a gentle hug and kiss, Jack waved and threw one more kiss as I headed for the highway. I pulled into one of my regular stops after an hour of driving. My neck was tired, and my head was heavy. The hamburger joint was only about two blocks down from the exit with a large store behind it. I stopped at the store first and walked around for about thirty minutes. I found some kid's books, like find-the-word and picture-in-the-picture. I purchased some of them in hopes of rehabilitating my brain. I was learning to read and write all over again; very frustrating! Back in the car again, I grabbed a burger and headed for the highway.

An hour later, I had to stop again. I couldn't make it to my next regular stop, so I pulled into another large store. After walking for half an hour I was back in the car and soon came to one of my favorite souvenir shops outside of Joplin, MO. I pulled into the parking lot, dodging the huge potholes. The jolt of hitting a pothole was pain I didn't need. Thankfully, there was parking near the front door. I carefully got out of the car and slowly stood. I had to stand for a few minutes until I could force my body to move.

I started stretching my lower back and shoulders. I walked around to the end of my car facing the trunk. I put one foot on the bumper and firmly planted the other in the gravel about a step behind me. I put my hands on the trunk, shifted my weight to the foot on the bumper and stretched my back leg in a backward arch from hip to toe. A couple of those on both sides and I was good to walk around.

I walked into the store and headed for the restroom and then walked around the store for half an hour. It gave my body a good stretch and allowed me time to look at all the treasures in the store. Handmade quilts, T-shirts and toys, moccasins, and homemade candy. One more restroom stop to splash my face and I headed out to the car. I opened my door and stretched for probably another ten or fifteen minutes. I noticed the ladies were watching me from inside the store; most likely wondering what on earth I was doing out there.

I eased myself into the driver's seat, trying to ignore the pain and spasms in my back. I wouldn't take pain meds and drive. When I hit the border at Bella Vista, AR, I stopped at the Traveler's Aid station. Inside I washed my face with cold water and looked at myself in the mirror. "You can do this, you can, you can do this. You're almost halfway there so you can stop soon for the night."

I was feeling spent and ready to lie down. I was long overdue for a horizontal break. Knowing I was less than an hour to the motel where I could finally lie down and ice kept me going.

I arrived at my hotel at about 6:00pm. Once inside my room, I phoned home to let Jack know where I was; that I was okay and would be icing. After my call, I hobbled down to the ice machine, filled up the bucket, and hobbled back to my room. I was done driving for the day, so I took my pain meds, iced for 30 minutes, then took a long hot shower to relax my stiff aching muscles. I phoned the local pizza joint for a delivery; a sausage and mushroom pizza almost always makes me feel better. I had the pillows in all the right places, and I sacked out on the bed with my pizza and watched TV. There was some comfort in knowing I was more than halfway there. I was getting concerned about how this trip would turn out.

With the morning came the sounds of all the cars starting up outside ready for their day. When I glanced at the clock it was only 6:30. I rolled back over and closed my eyes. Next thing I knew it was 8:30. I felt exhausted. Everything was stiff, everything hurt, and I had another 3 ½ hours of driving time left. I was in no real hurry to get into the car again. Outside I slowly lowered myself into the driver seat, turned the key, and was on my way. Traffic was heavier than I anticipated; full of trucks and semi's. I started to panic so I slowed down and let everyone go around me. I did not want to be that close to a group of cars. It was just too overwhelming.

After driving for an hour, my right leg was really hurting again. My left shoulder and right hip were really mad. Construction on the road was making me even tenser. I stopped every hour or less when I felt my body drawing up and tightening in pain or panic. I did my best to ignore my body screaming at me and kept driving until I got to Jesseville at around 4:00pm. I pulled off the highway and filled up my tank. I grabbed two more bags of ice, one at a time of course, and replenished the coolers. My friends' house was only about four miles away.

The day of driving had finally come to an end. When I arrived, I was greeted in the driveway by most of the family. They were aware of the wreck and my body's broken condition. They were so glad I made the trip and wouldn't let me lift anything. I pointed to the bag I needed for that section of my trip. Tomorrow we would be driving to Little Rock for the graduation and staying in a hotel. I was exhausted, cramping, and glad driving was done for the day. I lay down with my ice packs while Grace and I caught up with chit chat and enjoyed some fudge before bedtime.

When the morning came, I went through my morning ritual. A hot steamy shower to loosen up, rinsed my face with cold water, and a pep talk in the mirror…"you can do this." We loaded the cars and hit the road with an hour ride ahead of us. My right leg had been cramping since I got up and, after thirty minutes of driving, the pain was almost agony.

As we neared the city, signs were everywhere, "road work ahead." I panicked inside; there were orange barrels as far as the eye could see. My grip on the steering wheel tightened, and I had trouble breathing. I was thankful Grace was in the car; she knew where we were going. We bobbed and weaved around obstacles until we reached our off-ramp, my knuckles still white from clutching the wheel.

We finally arrived at the hotel and checked in. We went to our rooms and took an hour off before heading over to Faith's apartment to deal with any last minute details. Faith would be receiving her Master's degree that night. It was held in a beautiful old building with marvelous glass windows; a lovely space. We were sitting on hard wooden pews in the upper balcony close to an exit so I could get up and have room to stretch. Those pews were so hard; mix that with a wreck, depression and pain, and you have the recipe for a cranky girl.

Excitement filled the air as the ceremony commenced. Flash cameras were everywhere; capturing the moments. The wooden pew I was sitting on was fast becoming a real pain in the butt; literally. I don't remember how long we sat there. I felt as if I'd driven for another four hours; so sore and tired I was afraid I wouldn't last.

After the ceremony, Grace and I looked around for Faith and let her know we were going to dinner and then back to the hotel. I felt dreadful. My neck felt like a slinky and my head was a bowling ball. When we got back to the hotel, I iced, took a hot shower, and cried. My body was so drained; I feared I wouldn't be able to make it home.

When morning came, I could barely move. I was cranky and felt horrible. Proud parents Grace and Henry stopped by my room early. They were going over to Faith's apartment before the big class graduation. I couldn't bear the thought of sitting in a stadium all day. I needed serious downtime. I had hinted at missing the stadium graduation last night so they weren't surprised when I told them I was staying at the hotel close to the ice machine. I was so happy the hotel had an ice maker on my floor. Hallelujah. I was even happier that I made the decision to stay horizontal at the hotel and skip the stadium. My head was banging, my butt was twanging, and my rib was pounding.

It was getting close to party time. I took a nice hot shower so I could move my major body parts. I wasn't driving, choosing instead to take a cab so I could take my pain meds in hopes of enjoying the celebration. I had done so much driving in the last three days, my body was breaking down. It's amazing the impact driving has on the entire body. The cab was $8 well spent.

The afternoon slowly blended into dusk. People were folding blankets and putting up tables; packing for the trip home. I had a good time, but was feeling very droopy. I had no energy left. I was more than happy to go back to the hotel. I couldn't wait to ice down again and take a hot shower. I was cooked and I knew it, and yet I still heard that voice in my head saying, "I'm fine, I'm fine." I was still in denial anything was wrong, even with all the feedback from my body.

I had a long night of short naps and more ice. Morning came too soon. The muscles across my lower back felt like belted tires. I knew I had to get up, take a shower, get packed, and drive an hour back to Jessieville. I ignored the anxiety and trembling inside as I thought about all that construction. My body kept complaining; I was so very tired and drained, as if someone had unscrewed my ankles and all the energy ran out.

When the drive back to their house was finally over, we pulled into the driveway and began unpacking cars. We got everything settled inside; or I should say, "they" got everything settled. I wasn't much use and they wouldn't let me lift anything. I was grateful for another night of horizontal rest before the big drive home.

I am very thankful for my Arkansas family. I love them all so dearly! Sadly, I have not been able to make the drive to see them since.

In the morning I would be on the road and my way home to Jack. Excellent motivation for driving myself too hard, pardon the pun. When I woke, the negative mind chatter kicked in again and the left side of my neck was sore and stiff and wired directly to my tear ducts. I lay there, totally supported by the bed, gently rolling my head from side to side and telling it to relax. I was only driving halfway today, so I didn't start out until the afternoon. Everyone helped pack the car. I had my trusty coolers on the floorboards within reach. We said our goodbyes with gentle hugs, and I was on the road again. All I needed now was ice and gas.

I stopped for gas at a grab-n-go store right by the highway. I was moving slowly when I picked up the nozzle and put it in the tank. Pain shot through my chest. It felt like that swollen rib moved out of place from lifting the nozzle and my rib cage had unhooked. I put my hand at the base of my neck and used firm strokes to pull everything back down. Maybe this was a fascia thing. It hurt really badly when my chest felt disconnected like that. I never had this problem before the wreck.

When the car was full, I slowly put the nozzle back in its place with both hands. The coolers were full of ice and ready to go. Enough stalling; it was time to hit the road. Settled in my car, I took a left onto the highway and was on my way home. Dan Fogelberg and John Denver were close at hand to keep me company on the road. I plugged in "Home Free" by Fogelberg and listened to "To the Morning," a great song to start the drive off, even though it was afternoon. Listening to music I knew and could sing along to helped me drive; it helped me deal with the other drivers I just couldn't trust.

The first hour of driving was mostly through pouring rain. My right leg, especially my calf, was in grave pain. There was a growing knot between my shoulders, and my left shoulder was cramping up. My body forced me to stop driving after an hour to get out and stretch. My body would chime in frequently and demand, "You'd better stand up now." I was exhausted. I wanted to be home.

Even with stretch breaks, my body was pretty uncomfortable. I kept driving, wanting to be home so badly. I stopped for the night at a hotel in Carthage, MO. More ice bags and then another hot shower and pizza delivery. I slept in the next morning, even with all the traffic noise. I had a noon check out and I took advantage of that. I felt like crap; my shoulders, my neck, my right leg, pretty much all over. I did my stretches, and had yet another hot shower. I was so tired. There was more rainy weather in the forecast and I wasn't looking forward to that.

I drove through another hour of rain and then stopped to stretch for about half an hour. I could feel how close I was to home. Finally I saw a sign for Kansas City. I was excited and exhausted, like the agony and the ecstasy. Another thirty miles and I would be home. I had been so afraid I wouldn't be able to make the drive back home. When I finally pulled in the driveway and parked, I took a nice deep breath. Jack met me in the driveway. I opened my door and he offered his arm so I could pull myself up out of the car. Everything was stiff and sore, especially my lower back. My shoulders and hips felt like I had been carrying an eighty pound backpack. Everything would be fine, I was home.

"Welcome home," Jack gave me a kiss and a gentle hug and helped me into the house. "I love you. I'm glad you're home. I missed you woman!"

"I love you too. It's so good to be home."

"You go pour yourself into a hot shower, and I'll get the car unpacked."

"Not a problem," I said. "Will you help me get these clothes off?" I could feel the tears coming.

"I thought you would never ask," Jack said with a smile in

his eyes. I turned on the water and Jack helped me out of my clothes. I carefully stepped into the shower. The hot water felt fabulous on my poor tattered body. As my body warmed up from the heat, I started doing some gentle stretches to see if everything could still move. I could hear Jack digging in the ice, fixing ice packs for me.

When I came out of the bathroom, he smiled and said, "Your sheets have been changed, and the bedroom is ready for you." Is he cool, or what? I slowly wobbled and hobbled up the stairs. Jack followed behind me with the ice packs and a towel in tow. He made sure I was comfortable and had ice packs on both ends. Then he handed me the TV binky. "I will check on you later," he said. I turned on the TV and think I was asleep in 10 minutes. I didn't see Jack until I woke up the next morning, stiff and sore all over. Jack told me to take the day off and rest, so I did.

All that driving broke my "sitter." You know the group of muscles you use when you sit down and sit up? I call them my "sitter." They were on strike. I would spend days horizontal, until they had had plenty of time to rest and recuperate.

"Nothing in the world can take the place of persistence."
~ Calvin Coolidge (1872—1933)

Chapter 12

Sweat Suits in Summer, Ice Ice Ice

Every day, ice, ice, and more ice; months of ice, twenty minutes on and twenty minutes off, day after day. I think my "normal" body temperature dropped fifteen degrees from all the ice. Ice and steamy showers are two of my best friends. The ice helps with swelling and inflammation, and it numbs the pain. Then a hot steamy shower helps loosen all of the body's muscles. I'd stand in the shower, hot water aimed at my lower back. I'd close my eyes and give thanks for the invention of the hot shower and for the ability to move and stand. Things began to loosen up as I moved my limbs around in the hot steamy water, and I was able to move again for a short time.

Somewhere during this time, I remembered how many "tools" I had in my toolbox. I've been studying energy techniques for more than 20 years. Looking back, it's odd I didn't realize that sooner. Then again, my brain was like applesauce. I pulled out my Repatterning books to see what I could do for myself to quicken the healing process. Using a six step process, Repatterning makes the unknown known and uses modalities to shift resonance with the issues keeping us stuck in limitation. I very quickly became aware of the fact that I could not read. I could see letters and I could see words, but nothing meant anything and that really creeped me out.

The first summer after the wreck was cold and frustrating. It took two weeks to figure out a simple beanpole trellis. I'd watch gardening shows and have no understanding of what they were doing. It was like the mechanic in my head flew out of my left ear that day and splattered on the pavement. I went outside on beautiful summer days already knowing I wouldn't get to play in the dirt, but I did try to make myself go outside. I knew it was good for me, and I had always loved being outside.

I began to love my little container garden. It makes that little spot feel so plush. It could be a nice, warm, sunny day, a hundred degrees in Midwest humidity, and I always had on a sweat suit and socks because I was always freezing.

I had no brain left for reading or writing, so I began to teach myself to write again, and the headaches were always there. I started practicing the alphabet in capitals and then in lowercase, like in grade school. My letters took up three lines on wide lined paper. It felt like I practiced writing capital and lowercase letters for years. Once the letters were mastered, I had to learn how to write words. I still flipped my letters and misspelled a lot of words. It was so strange. I couldn't get what was in my head out of my mouth or onto paper. My brain and body were betraying me. I was locked in denial. Okay, so I was in a car wreck; it's been months, and I should be better by now.

Even months later, as my reading improved, I had great difficulty reading out loud. I no longer had the smooth, fluid, nurturing voice I had before the wreck. I stuttered when speaking. My voice lacked me, no bounce at all, more like profound sorrow. I began reading everything aloud to practice a "natural" voice. The issues I had with speaking made everything harder. It was embarrassing. It was not my voice. It wasn't a soothing voice I could use with clients.

"Do what you can, with what you have, where you are."
~ Theodore Roosevelt (1858 – 1919)

Chapter 13

Physical Therapy in the Fall

I told my MD's office several times that I wanted an MRI, but they wouldn't order one. During one visit I was told I could have the MRI if I agreed to go in for a spinal injection. I refused that "deal." I was outraged, it felt like medical blackmail! I did some research on spinal injections and asked opinions of people I respect. I did meet a few people they worked for, but it was an option of last resort for me. I saw no reason to pump steroids into my spine until I knew exactly what was causing the pain.

Nine months after the wreck, my doctors Gallo and Sebastian thought I was finally ready for the rigors of physical therapy (PT). Dr. Sebastian once told me, "I think traditional medicine sometimes sends people to PT too soon. There are a lot of tears and the muscles need time to heal. Going to physical therapy the week after your wreck may have made your condition a lot worse. After being tossed around in the car, there's no doubt you had micro-tears throughout your whole body, and your fascia was a mess. Chances are in your case, had they put you into PT a week after your wreck, it would have stressed the muscles more, and caused more injury to the fascia, and you would be using a lot more ice."

When I went back to my MD's office, instead of pushing spinal injections, the doctor finally suggested PT. That I could do. I received more information and I set up the appointment.

I was nervous about my first visit to PT. My referral diagnosis from my MD was neck, shoulder, right hip pain, and headaches. When I arrived, there was another stack of papers to fill out. When the paperwork was done, I met my physical therapist.

"Hi, I'm Cal; I'll be your physical therapist. Today I'll do an evaluation and assess your condition, and then I can put together the best treatment plan for you."

The evaluation was filled with, "move this way" and "move that way." When I pulled something, it felt okay; when I pushed, it hurt.

"So do you feel worse in the morning or in the evening?"

"The morning," I responded.

"Feeling achy in the morning is pretty normal. The nerves need time to heal, and so does the rib. From my evaluation, I don't feel you have a disc problem. But you have lost your glide."

My forehead wrinkled as I looked at him sideways, puzzled. "What is a glide?"

He explained how "nerves run all over the body. During the trauma of the car wreck, your nerves contracted, just like a muscle does. Those nerves need to be stretched out again so they glide with your body as it moves, like they are supposed to."

"Do you think I had a concussion?"

"I have no doubt you had a concussion; that's usually a given with whiplash."

"So why would my MD think I didn't have one, just because I don't remember if I hit my head?"

"When you don't take a direct hit to head it is usually referred to as a contrecoup injury. More than likely, your brain was pretty bruised after spinning around inside your skull."

"Wow," I thought to myself, he gets it like Dr. Gallo does. Nerve glide made sense. The nerve glide was like the fascia work, just with a different focus. This is good.

He was ready to move on. "We will start with exercises to stretch the nerves back out first. I can feel by the way your arms move that the nerves have lost their glide. Moving your arm up and down, like doing a bicep curl, the nerves should glide easily as the arm moves. Yours feel stuck and most likely filled with trauma."

One exercise for glide was to sit in a 90° angle, my legs flat out in front and my back straight. The movement was simple and painful. All I had to do was bend my head forward and backward. When I bent my head forward I could feel the pull all the way down to the middle of my back. Proof once again that it's all connected. I still couldn't bend my head backward.

Another exercise also great for the posture, the "shoulder pinch", with shoulders lowered and relaxed, pulling the shoulders back, squeezing between the shoulder blades. This strengthened the shoulders and brought the stress back down to the shoulder where it belonged, instead of lodging in the neck.

About an hour after my appointment, the right side of my neck and the back of my head really hurt! Once again, I felt the evils of evaluation. Every time I have been evaluated, everything gets all stirred up, and I feel like crap for the rest of the week.

When I got home, I used the heating pad and then napped for about three hours. This became an evaluation ritual.

The next morning I was sore. I added the new PT exercises to the ones I was already doing and took a nice shower to steam myself so everything would loosen up and move. I had an appointment with Dr. Gallo at noon and, boy, was I looking forward to it. I felt like there was a fist pushing against my mid-back area. She said my back felt a bit looser. When she adjusted me, I could feel the gentle pop where the fist had been. The top of my head hurt, but that eased within an hour. That night I was asleep by ten.

The second PT appointment started with the three exercises I had already suffered through at home that morning. Then my therapist added two more exercises for the shoulders using rubber therapy bands. Next, I had my first encounter with traction, commonly known as the rack. PT was quickly changing from Physical Therapy to Pain and Torture.

Lying on a long metal table, he strapped me in. It was like a neck brace with a headband attached. This gave the machine the ability to stretch me in the right direction, while maintaining stability in my neck. The first time I was on the traction table, I heard a big pop deep inside my neck. It felt like something stuck had popped loose. By the end of my appointment, I was completely drained. I rested for a few hours before I did my exercises again. The new band exercises immediately fatigued the muscles in my back and neck, and my legs shook when I straightened them while performing my new exercises.

The weeks in PT dragged on, each week adding one or two more exercises. The pain would shift all over my body. I would get so frustrated because the PT protocol did not address the body as a whole. You're parted out like a car. The days were long and the nights were even longer. I had gotten to the point when I could tell my head was in the wrong place. I would go to Dr. Gallo and say, "put my head back on straight," literally, as usual.

As the weeks went on, part of me was starting to feel stronger while new problems surfaced from the therapy exercises. Therapy had me up and stretching; that was more than I had been able to do in months. It seemed, no matter what I did, I had pain in my lower back. If I picked something up, did the dishes, or typed for too long, my shoulders would burn inside. I still couldn't make hamburger patties. You know when you make a giant meatball and then press it flat with one hand on each side? Still can't do it. It makes my rib hurt. So does scrubbing, and pushing down on the counter with a rag. I can't lift. I still can't do things with my arms out in front of me like washing the dishes or typing. It was amazing how much my life had changed in an instant, so many months ago. I really missed my life. Now this was my life, no matter how I tried to deny it.

I was going to PT and the chiropractor, still getting massage and CranioSacral therapy. I did feel a little better. I had okay days but more not okay days. There was a cold rainy day in early October. I had been in PT for about three weeks. It was amazing, I felt like a weather machine. The lower the barometric pressure got, the worse I felt. Dr. Sebastian said "Everyone is different. For some when the pressure is high, their pain got worse and, for you, it's when it gets low."

I had a new respect for people who trust their knees when they say a storm's coming. They're usually right, aren't they? Actually, now that I think about it, it might be easier to have my knees tell me there is a storm coming instead of my whole body. It would get bad; the base of my skull felt like it would explode, as opposed to the headache I got when I knew my head had fallen off my body, and I needed Dr. Gallo to put it back on straight. Both chiropractors noticed a difference with the PT. So could my massage and CranioSacral practitioners. When I did my exercises, I was exhausted. The only difference I felt was that I was always really tired. My physical therapist told me that after three or four weeks I would get that endorphin rush from doing the exercises that would make me feel great. Then I would want to keep up the exercises...That never happened.

I went to PT two or three times a week, increasing my workout as we went. I was befuddled that he only worked on one area of my body. It's all connected! Why doesn't the protocol allow for this? Why would you work on the right shoulder and not the left shoulder? Healing is about balance, and working only one side of the body left me feeling unbalanced after my appointment. When I did my exercises at home, I always did them on both sides.

One afternoon I was at home stretching with one of my Chi Gung tapes; gentle movement that stimulates the body and the "chi" or "life force energy." Later I was trying to move my right arm in a circle simply moving my right arm from hanging straight down to making a nice flowing circle above my head and then back around to hanging straight again. My right arm was not following the process. Since I know the body is all connected, I thought I would teach the right arm with the left arm. I talked to my right arm. I said, "Okay right arm, watch the left arm." And then I would talk to my left arm saying, "Show my right arm how to make a circle." My body knew what I was asking. My left arm began making a slow circle.

Starting with my left arm hanging down straight, I would move it up and over my head, and then back around to its original position. I made circles with my left arm for five minutes. I kept telling my right arm to pay attention. When I tried to make a circle with my right arm, I had trouble lifting it above shoulder height and the circle backwards was actually more out to the side and back down to my leg again. I repeated this process for several days. Finally the right arm was able to make a better circle! It still would not go very far above my head, and on the backward swing down, it was barely behind the center of my body, but all in all, good progress I thought.

I was so aware of what my body was capable of doing before the accident that I frustrated my therapist. I always asked questions. "What is this for? What does that do?" He introduced a new exercise where you pull the shoulders up to your ears and look up at the ceiling, then let the shoulders drop and the head comes back into position.

I asked him, "Where's the rest of the exercise?"

He was bewildered, "what do you mean the *rest* of the exercise?"

"After you drop your shoulders and your head comes back into position, you push the head back just enough to get a little traction in the neck for a stretch." It was obvious he had never seen this before.

"It's called the turtle neck release. It's a modality I learned in Resonance Repatterning years ago. I must frustrate you at times; I probably know more about my body than most of the people you work with."

"I would say you know more than 95% of the people I work with."

"I used to teach classes in sound and movement. I am totally aware of what my body could do before the wreck, and what it still can't do now. I miss my old body. Will it ever be the same?" There was no response. There was never a response.

PT was scheduled on a four-week basis. Every four weeks I would be re-evaluated, and it was always painful. After the re-evaluation, notes were sent to my MD, along with the therapist's recommendations. She would renew my prescription for PT. Altogether I spent about four months in PT, that time.

I was surprised how expensive PT is, even on days when they plop you on a machine, set the timer, and off they go to someone else. At first I felt abandoned. Self-pity would rush into my head, "I am paying for your time, so why aren't you spending your time with me when I am here? I'm broken and you walked away."

I continued with physical therapy and started feeling stronger. Once I learned my exercises it didn't bother me anymore when he walked away. I understood that like any other discipline, PT has its own protocol. I think the biggest gift is learning which exercises to do for what, and in what order to do them. I remember getting bills listing "manual manipulation." I guess that was for whenever he touched me, putting on electrodes or ice. I know I never received a massage there. Every little charge has to have a reason. That's because insurance companies decide what is covered and what is not. It's like the doctor in the emergency room who didn't run tests. I had nothing broken, and nothing was bleeding, so what was there to test?

I am grateful for PT because it did help. It took me years to own the fact that I had to keep doing those specific movements. When I experimented with other types of workouts I had used in the past, I felt weaker inside. Sometimes, my old routines would even hurt me. I have come to learn, no matter what exercise I tried to see if my body could handle it, I have to keep up with the targeted PT exercises to keep my body in motion. Years later, when I was whining about having to keep doing PT forever, a friend said, "Why don't you just stop calling it PT and just call it "your exercises." That sounded so much better. If you do your PT "exercises" right, it is quite a workout.

It was very frustrating: I would start feeling better, almost like my old self again; I could do more things, and I wanted it to *stay* that way. Several times I'd forget to do my PT exercises because I felt good. After all, since I had done my work and felt better, I should stay better, right? But then after about a week, my body started seizing up again. One day I could barely move because everything was seizing up. I'd be in bed for a week. My body was telling me the PT "exercises" were a must to keep feeling better. It had been screaming at me and I wasn't listening. The four-year-old inside of me would throw tantrums because she couldn't do anything. I admit that no matter what I did, or how good I felt, I still had to take at least one or two days off a week to rest horizontally. Many times I was down a whole week.

When I was gathering up all my medical reports, I was amazed at what they all contained. My physical therapy records would start with a sheet with a diagnosis above, and then list the objectives and goals for the patient. On my final session of PT, it read, "All objectives completed, patient still complains of pain." We had reached the "objectives" that could be dealt with through physical therapy. It did help with some of the pain, and I was feeling a bit stronger. Their goals were met. I had met the maximum benefit their facility could deliver within their realm of practice.

During my time in PT, I did draw out my exercises. Going two times a week doesn't mean I remember the exercises when I get home. All it takes is your thumb pointing down instead of up during an exercise to make things worse.

I was still in pain, so my objectives weren't complete. And yes, I was still icing. I was better, but I still had more bad days than good days. My lower back would still spasm. When walking, an area on my lower right side would suddenly go weak and I felt like I would collapse. I complained about that pain from the start.

"The cure of the part should not be attempted
without the cure of the whole."
~ Plato (c. 428/427 BC – c. 428/427 BC)

Chapter 14

The Sin of Soft-Tissue Injury

Gladly we both had insurance; in our state, it's the law. The lady who hit me openly apologized to me and told the police that she didn't see me. There was no question of fault, so I would file my claim with her insurance company. I remembered back to the day after the wreck when we got home from the chiropractor, there was a phone message. Mike Hill from her insurance company left his information and asked that I return his call.

I was a mess when I called him back. I was high on bodywork, pain, and painkillers. I remembered how he convinced me that everything would be fine. "She is covered. We will pay for the damage to your car. We will pay for your medical bills, cover your lost wages, and look at pain and suffering." He was so nice. I fell for it...hook, line, and sinker. In hindsight, I wish Jack had talked to him.

But then as the weeks crept on, I kept getting worse. I called Mike at her insurance company to let him know I was getting worse, and I needed to change doctors. He told me to get the help I needed. He even sounded concerned. That was when I started seeing Dr. Gallo. It was about a month after the wreck.

Within six months I received a call from her insurance company asking if I was ready to settle for $5,800. That wouldn't even cover my lost wages. My heart began to pound. I started crying. I felt a panic attack coming on. I took some deep breaths and called Tracy, my paralegal friend. I spoke through my sniffles, "The insurance company called and they're trying to bully me into settling for $5,800. That's ridiculous."

"Calm down, take a breath, there is nothing to settle until you have been medically released. If they continue to stress you out and make you cry like this, stop talking to them. You can always answer their letter with a letter telling them you're still under medical care. Be a broken record. Until you are released there is nothing to settle, so calm down."

"I could call after the office closes and leave a message."

"That would work."

I instantly panic every time the insurance people call. I still can't believe how bad they make me feel. Their settlement offer was $5,800. What an insult! A year later the offer was the same. When I told the insurance adjuster that my medical bills were pushing $30,000 and that their offer wouldn't even pay my lost wages, he said, "It doesn't matter how many doctors you see, this is the only offer you will get."

My jaw dropped. I was speechless, just for a moment, and then I blurted out, "I have a follow-up with the neurologist next week."

"It doesn't matter. Our offer is $5,800 and that won't change," he replied coldly.

I remember when I was sent back to physical therapy by the pain management doctor. The bookkeeper said she called the insurance company and talked with an adjuster. "I wanted to know if the paperwork we have will cover this time around or if we have to start a new set because it's a new calendar year. He told me he didn't know if insurance would pay for any of this, because you turned down an offer in December."

"Yeah, right," I said with disgust. "They offered me $5,800. That's no offer; that's what it cost to fix my car! What a jerk!" Now he was trying to intimidate my health care provider. Oh, I was so angry! I don't know if it was legal for him to discuss my case.

We started a new set of papers and my next round of physical therapy began. I'd forgotten that the agreement with physical therapy required payment within twenty-seven months so they would be paid, whether I received a settlement or not. That was over two years away; I thought the wreck would be settled before then.

Interestingly, the insurance company doesn't pay your bills. They pay a lump sum when you are ready to settle. All my doctor appointments were paid by my own health insurance or out of our pocket. My health insurance company filed a lien with the auto insurance company because they wanted their money and there were two other liens from doctors. A measly $5,800 was not nearly enough to pay them back, so there was no point in settling, even if I had been released.

The insurance company is so huge and has so much money, they can outlast just about anyone. When you don't settle fast, they patiently wait for you to get desperate so you will settle for pennies. Sadly, too often, soft-tissue injuries are ignored. It's not like a broken bone or a bloody knee you can see and treat. Soft-tissue includes everything that's not bone. Torn fascia is a serious soft-tissue injury no one can see. A concussion is a soft-tissue injury no one can see. Your body is mostly soft-tissue; irreplaceable and priceless.

We were filing with the other driver's insurance company because the accident was her fault. (This all varies by state). Now her insurance company was trying to minimize my injuries and their worth. How do you put a price on someone's life and health, especially knowing that a person's life and health will never be the same? I worry sometimes that insurance companies will lobby and win to cap settlements no higher than the cost to fix your car. Paying stockholders seems to be more important than paying claims. So, the smaller the payout, the more money there is to keep the stockholders happy.

One day, on the trip to the MD's office, I was freaking out, as usual, and Jack was driving. I was in a weepy mood. My voice was quivering when I asked Jack, "What if they can't fix me?" Tears were rolling down my face and my nose was starting to run.

Jack was quiet for a minute and then said, "Honey, you are not a car. You're an organic body, and you will heal. It takes as long as it takes. It's not like you're a car and they can bang out the fenders and replace the doors."

"What if this is the best I get?" I felt like such a burden.

Jack put his hand on my knee as I wiped my face dry. "Stop worrying so much. It's not helping you. It won't help get you better. It'll take as long as it takes. Think of all the things you can do now that you couldn't do six months ago." My mind went blank trying to remember what I can do now. I couldn't think of anything. I still couldn't make a hamburger patty. I still can't get a great hug from Jack. I couldn't even kiss very long. When I bend my neck sideways it hurts my neck and starts a debilitating headache. Touch is so important for the human soul.

My injuries touched every aspect of my life. Good touching

and hugging with Jack became rare because it was so painful to be touched. There came a point when Jack was afraid to touch me for fear of hurting me. For all the pain and sorrow I had been through, it's ridiculous that they only offered me $5,800 to cover everything when my medical bills were pushing $30,000. I wanted my life and my time back, but they couldn't fix that, and money won't replace it.

I spoke with my insurance agent, and he told me that the amount paid for pain and suffering was generally twice the medical bills. I doubt he would repeat that. The legal world says there is no formula. My insurance agent was the only person who told me not to get a lawyer involved. "They just mess up the works." The other insurance company had become gruff and told me, "You have the right to get an attorney."

My agent referred me to the insurance commissioner's office. He told me they would open a case and look into the offer I was made. I called them several times. The first time the woman who answered didn't want to help me. I told her what my medical bills were and what their offer was and that I needed help. She responded, "If you're trying to get more money out of them, you'll have to get a lawyer. There's nothing I can do for you," and the call ended.

I called the Insurance Commissioner's office again four months later. This time the person on the other end of the phone at least seemed interested. I told her the story of the wreck and when and how it happened. She asked if I had filed for disability yet. I said, "No, I didn't know that I could."

"Honey, that's the first thing you need to get done; you file for that disability. There are time limits on when you can file. Someone should have told you that before now so you could get that paperwork in." I thanked her for the information and wished her a good day. That was the best piece of advice I got from the Insurance Commissioner's office. There would still be no case opened.

All the stress and all that time wasted. I could have filed for help from disability years ago? Because the woman that hit me left the country, months of Case Management Conferences were always postponed. Why is that my problem? She paid her premiums, so pay up already. Her insurance company had no interest in finding her. If she never showed up or contacted them she could be classified as a non-cooperative client and they might have a way to wiggle out of the settlement. (This likely also varies by state).

"Slow and steady wins the race."

~ Aesop (620 BC - 560 BC)

Chapter 15

Applying for Disability

It was now over four years, two lawyers, and almost 250 medical visits since the wreck, and I just found out I had the option to file for disability. Why was this the first time I remembered it being mentioned? In all fairness, someone may have told me to file but, with my brain damage, I don't remember it if they did.

I went online to www.socialsecurity.gov, clicked on the disability tab, and slowly started reading. I'm grateful that a woman at the Insurance Commissioner's office told me to file. In the reading I found the rules and points and how they figure it out, and I only had about 4 months left to apply.

I started the online filing that day. It was overwhelming. Fortunately, the website allowed me to log in and out of the application process, so I was able to take breaks, which was good because they wanted a lot of information and I couldn't sit comfortably for more than fifteen minutes at a time. They wanted everything. What happened? What's your condition now? List your doctors and other medical professionals, hospitals, and clinics. What meds are you on? What medical tests did you have done? Then it was how do your problems interfere with your work? List all of your job history and what you did. Then it moved into education and training. Then there were medical release forms so they could request my medical records. It seemed to go on forever! When it was finally done, I printed everything and looked it over carefully. Then I looked it over again, and yet again. I was worried I might have missed something. I took a big gulp and hit "submit." There was no going back now. All that thinking gave me a pounding headache, and I was exhausted.

I packed up my medical records, had copies made and then drove to the local Social Security office. The lady behind the counter looked very confused, even though I had the name of the person who was to receive the records. She took them to somewhere behind the curtain. When she returned, she flashed a quick smile and said, "They will be taken care of." I thanked her, turned and headed for the car and went on home.

A month later I received a form letter listing my answers from my input on their web application. Also enclosed were a copy of the "Paperwork Reduction Act" and four copies of a function report. One was for me, one was for my husband, and the other two could be given to friends. There was an address to mail everything to so the information could be scanned in. Now I was confused. I had turned my records into the local office, as directed. I read through the paperwork again. I made another copy of my records, completed the function reports and mailed them, as directed. Another thinking headache attacked me.

Another six weeks crept by before I received correspondence. A very nice form letter told me I had been denied disability. Many friends warned me I would be turned down the first time. The letter stated that, to be eligible, I had to have impairments that kept me from working for twelve months, or impairments that would result in death. I hadn't been able to work for four years so I don't understand why I was denied. I wondered if they even looked at my records. My eyes were wet as I read all the information. I had 60 days to file an appeal, so I logged on and immediately filed for an appeal, which meant a hearing in front of a judge.

Another month had dragged by when I received the next form letter thanking me for my request to schedule a hearing. It explained the process for my hearing in front of an Administrative Law Judge (ALJ). I would be notified at least twenty days before the hearing. It explained my rights to choose representation and, should I retain a lawyer, they could charge no more than the fee allowed by the court.

It would be another year of court dates, scheduled and rescheduled, and another new lawyer hand-off for the insurance settlement, before I would receive the letter setting a court date for my disability appeal with the judge.

"The strongest of all warriors are these two — Time and Patience."

~ Leo Tolstoy (1828 – 1910)

Chapter 16

Patience Little Jackass

I think I survived my ordeal because I found my sense of humor. It was difficult learning to ask for help, and ultimately, accepting the fact that I can't do it all myself. What's wrong with asking for help? "Nothing," said the tortoise.

I am blessed to be best friends with my Mom. She supported me the entire time the circus ran its course, and as I wrote this book. One time, hiding out at her house after a deposition, she helped me through a severe panic attack with distraction. She asked if I was all right, and I told her, "I don't know if I'm having a heart attack or a panic attack. I don't feel right."

After asking all the appropriate questions, she replied, "I don't think it's a heart attack, honey. I think it's a panic attack. I think this whole damn thing has gone on too long and you are worn out. This should have been settled years ago." She sounded as disgusted as I felt about all of it.

"If this is a panic attack, I'll take my meds. That's what they are there for."

I popped two pills and did my best to breathe. My mother began to distract me. She took me back to funny childhood memories, like fishing and feeding the minnows to the dog. My brother talking into his square metal trashcan and sounding just like Darth Vader! The time my other brother got his head stuck in the railing. That one really got me laughing; my head fit through the railing just fine. I looked at Mom and said, "I know what you're doing, please keep going."

"How about the hole in the wall under that poster in the hall?"

I laughed again. Here all these years later I had always believed she knew nothing about that hole.

No doubt the meds helped, but Mom was distracting me right out of my panic attack. The more I laughed, the calmer I felt. This is a good tool for the caretakers out there. Distraction can be a great tool when applied properly and at the right time.

"Patience Little Jackass" has been a term of endearment between us for years. Funny thing, it's the punch line to a joke no one remembers. Humor and laughter are so important! They will always lift your vibration. If you don't feel like laughing, laugh anyway. Your brain doesn't know the difference.

One time Mom and I were driving to the store and Mom said, "How about a steak Sunday?"

I thought that was odd, such a visual in my head. I said, "Why would you put ice cream on a steak?"

"Not a steak sundae, a steak Sunday." I was confused. I had to think about it for a few minutes. That's the soft-tissue brain damage. I did finally get it, and we still laugh about it.

Keep humor in your toolbox. There will be days you won't want to take it out and that's okay. There will be other days when you can't wait to pull it out and laugh. It took me years to figure this one out. As Lord Byron said, "Always laugh when you can. It is cheap medicine."

"Patience is bitter, but its fruit is sweet."
~ Aristotle (384 BC – 322 BC)

Chapter 17

Be a Broken Record

It was not even a year after the wreck, and the nice insurance guy no longer existed. Now he wanted me to settle and his demeanor had turned to intimidation. Hearing his voice on the answering machine, and the thought of calling him back, always filled me with debilitating anxiety.

When I returned his call, I always hoped he would be away from his desk so I could leave a message and avoid the confrontation. I had no desire to reach him only to be attacked. The anxiety from the memory of being bullied by this guy was overwhelming. I felt my heart sink; I had no energy. I felt like my beanie hat had run out of wind. The insurance company was making this more painful than the actual wreck.

Tracy and I had talked about this. She always said, "Be a broken record like they are when they offer you that ridiculous amount. There's nothing to settle yet, there is no case until you are medically released."

Every time they called, they had an excuse. One time a woman called; she was filling in for the insurance adjuster while he was on vacation. He had left the name of a doctor he wanted me to see for an examination. I remember Tracy had said, "Don't ever go to one of their doctors for treatment. You have the right to choose your own doctors. They can force the issue if they want and order an Independent Medical Exam, but they can't tell you who can treat you."

I told the woman I had my own doctors and would not be seeing theirs. After all, their doctor was working for them.

"Sometimes when things are falling apart,
they may actually be falling into place."
~ Author Unknown

Chapter 18

Finding the Groove
for Your New Moves

Learn to celebrate the victories of every day. Before the wreck, I had a pretty active social life. I chat more on the phone than visit in person these days. I love to sing, but since the wreck, I don't sing much, because when I do, I get a horrible headache. My body and brain no longer work the way they used to. I've had to experiment with new ways of movement and stillness. It was a matter of finding out what worked best for me. Necessity is the mother of invention and each person will find the formula that works best for them. Be grateful for what you do have, and continue your PT stretches even after your visits are complete. The body needs to move to continue to move. As they say, "Use it or lose it."

My intention for this chapter is to give people options they may not have tried before, or ever heard of, sparking a memory of a movement or exercise that makes life better. I hope you will find tidbits in this chapter that make your life, or the life of someone you love, easier.

By now you already know that I love hot showers to loosen up my muscles. When I wasn't able to stand long enough for a shower, I used the heating pad to "iron" my muscles. Always remember heat and ice. When the ice is just too cold, put the heating pad on your feet. Ask your doctor, find what works for you.

I have a grand collection of heating pads. One is like a short cape that covers my shoulders and my neck. A king size heating pad, two foot by one foot that covers my back, neck to sacrum. The next is for my lower back and hips. It connects in front with hook and loop material so there is no slipping whether I am lying down or sitting up. The latest addition to my collection is a lightweight shawl. The heated area is about twenty inches by thirty-two inches. The front panels are about fourteen inches with pockets but no heat. It's great, so light and supple I can apply it anywhere.

I also have a nice collection of ice packs. One that fits the contour of my neck, two standard size packs about eleven by fourteen inches, one jumbo size pack at twelve by eighteen inches, and two small ones about five by seven inches. They live in the freezer and are ready when I need them. I wrap them in pillowcases or a thin towel before applying them to wherever I need them. I am so use to ice packs that I rarely squeal anymore. I found a king size pillow case is long enough to fit the long contoured ice pack for my neck with room to secure it in front with a hair clip, making it much easier to keep in place.

I have had to keep my hair short because it gets so heavy my neck can't hold it up. It helps to stabilize my head with one hand, use the other hand to shampoo, and then switch off hands. I invested in a kick-ass blow dryer so all I need is one hand to wave the dryer around my head. I can switch hands as often as needed. I rarely style my hair anymore, I surrendered to my hair and all is well.

I miss sitting cross-legged on the floor for projects and sitting up in bed to watch TV. It still makes my lower back hurt and soon reminds me to stop sitting that way. Now I sit with my legs straight out in front, leaning on tall pillows behind me, or "uncrossed." I adapted to uncrossed from crossed-legged by pulling my knees out until the soles of my feet meet. My legs almost form a diamond shape. This change in position puts less stress on the pelvis and the sacroiliac (SI) joint. It works really well, when I remember to do it. Surprisingly, it's still not a habit. When I sit cross-legged, my body quickly reminds me to uncross.

The bottom shelves at the store can be a real bugger, and it's best for me not to reach, but there are things I need, and sometimes I just can't avoid it. It's best for me to squat to pick things up, whether it's from the bottom shelf at the store or just picking something up off the floor. Squats aren't leaning over but they get you lower. Bend your knees and bring your shoulders over the knees, over the feet. It's like sitting in a chair without the chair. Check with your health care professional to make sure squats are appropriate for you.

I have the same issues reaching for something high up in a cabinet. Over time, I came to learn a new way to reach up. When I looked up and reached with my arm, I had horrible pain in my neck and shoulders. Now I look up and find what I am looking for, then I look down and reach up with my arm and it works; almost pain free! Sounds odd but it works!

I have never totally regained my balance. I can be pretty wobbly on stairs especially when my hands are full. One thing I have found extremely helpful is having a bag at the bottom of the stairs and another one at the top. I load them with things that need to be moved from one level of the house to the other. This way, my hands are not full of things, and I can easily carry them from one floor to the other using only one hand to carry the bag and one hand for the railing. It works out great!

I missed what my body could do before, and many days I got frustrated or angry. Day by day new methods of movements evolved as I taught myself to adapt and move with my new body. I know it helps me and my caretakers to remember that sometimes I get irritable and short tempered, and it has nothing to do with them; it's me. Don't take it personally when I hide in my cave.

Communication with those around you is so important. They can't read your mind. They can't help you if you don't tell them what you need. I have had anxiety attacks ever since the wreck, and although I try I can't control them. When I am in a dreadful mood, I tell Jack and let him know it's not him so he won't spend the evening wondering if he did something wrong. I did that even before the wreck. I think it's great advice for any couple, dealing with a disaster or not.

Once on a family trip with Mom, my cousin picked us up in a huge black SUV. Going through the airport traffic, I began sucking in air and holding my breath. It was as if every inch we traveled without being hit surprised me. My cousin noticed right away. He said sternly, "This is my town and I know this airport, so stop worrying."

There were so many cars around us I was having trouble catching my breath. I told him, "It's me, it's not you. I was in a bad car wreck. I can't help it. All these cars freak me out. It's not you, it's me."

"I gotcha," he softened. "I see how having a car wreck could make you jumpy."

"Ignore me, I can't help it. It's a new reflex I've developed from the wreck." If this sounds like you, let your loved ones know what's going on with you. When you identify what makes you feel anxious or panicky, let those around you know.

To be clear, I am not a medical doctor. I am not a medical anything. Ask your healthcare professional if these are right for you. If anything hurts—don't do it! That being said, here are some more moves to help with new grooves. If they work for you great; if they don't, that's okay too. I wanted to share some moves that helped me. You may already have some of your own. I hope these add to your options.

I coined the phrase, "Tai Chi dishes" in the earlier stages of recovery when I was learning how to move my body in completely new and different ways. The old ways didn't work for me anymore. Most of them really made my body hurt. I had to learn how to integrate with my new and difficult body, after the wreck.

One night when I was washing dishes, I exclaimed, "Tai Chi dishes!" After washing two plates, my left shoulder would get a burning feeling. I spread my feet about hips width and swayed my weight between my feet. I got two more plates done and had to stop. That burn was so painful, it was electric! Washing dishes had become an all-day event. Wash two plates at a time, and then break with ice.

When I do activities that require holding my arms out, like washing dishes or folding towels, I get a nasty burn going under my left shoulder blade; probably a combination of nerve problems and bursitis. That's the shoulder injured by the force of the seatbelt during the crash. I needed to learn new ways to move my arm.

The classic horse stance is easy to practice for those who can stand. For those who cannot stand, close your eyes and imagine what the stance would feel like. Stand with your feet about hip width apart, pointing your toes straight ahead. Now swivel on your heels slightly, moving your toes in about an inch. If you were standing on skis, they would cross in front of you.

Slightly bend your knees and you have it, hence the name horse stance. It's about the same position you are in when riding. You may feel some stretching in your legs until you are used to this stance. Start off slowly, and work up to longer periods of time.

I use either this stance or a wider squat for washing dishes. It still takes me hours to do a sink full, but this helps my shoulders. I have a double sink, so I place one foot centered in front of each sink. I do my best to remember to move back and forth using my knees and hips; it's a good opportunity for stretching. While standing there, tighten up your butt and thighs and suck in that tummy. Good old fashioned isometrics work. If I can't reach something without bending, I move my feet, no overstretching under penalty of severe pain. I can do a few lunges while the next batch of dishes soak. Incorporate stretches and exercise in your new lifestyle every day.

Another simple step that can work well for doing dishes, or just using the sink, is to open the cabinet door beneath your sink, and put one foot up. Remember to trade off frequently so both sides of your body get a break.

One more stance that may come in handy is the archer stance. The archer stance has one foot in front, toes facing forward, the other foot is angled roughly 45° out about a hip width behind your front foot. Balance your weight between your two feet.

It helps to practice the stances until you feel comfortable with them. Once you become accustomed to these stances, they can be applied to a variety of other activities. There's folding laundry, preparing meals, and tons of other activities you do while standing and using your arms.

One of my favorite cooking pots is a 5-quart Griswold Dutch oven from 1927. I couldn't lift it for years. That pot taught me it was okay to ask Jack for help. Seven years later, in a stubborn streak, I found a new way to lift it. Using a squat to lower myself, I took the lid off and moved that; another squat and I moved the bottom part of the pan. I could move it on a good day as long as I didn't move the whole pot at the same time, or move it more than once. It's good to acknowledge the smallest things as progress, and celebrate with a wa-hooo! Give yourself permission to ask for help when you need it. There is no shame in asking for help, so let that go!

I have always cooked and always done things by hand. Since the wreck I no longer have the strength or stamina to do things by hand. Power tools for the kitchen are amazing! I have acquired a great hand mixer, a stand mixer, and a food processor. It took three power tools to do what I used to do by hand. Don't buy cheap ones or you will have to replace them frequently. Buy good tools for your kitchen and they will treat you well.

Gardening has always been one of my joys, but my body can no longer take all the bending and stooping. I don't know that I will ever be able to control the tiller again; the lawnmower and weed eater are still off-limits. One day, when the shop vac was outside, I thought, "why not?" I found that with two tubes attached to the hose I can suck up the leaves and old debris from last year without bending at all. "Shop Vac Gardening" was born. Thankfully, Jack empties the vacuum container. If you are on your own, suck up smaller batches. Always take advantage of any wheels! Maybe put a small shop vac into a wagon. I can't weed the garden this way, but it sure helps with cleanup duties. It's wonderful to be outside, even if it's just to enjoy great weather.

My garden has been downsized to containers only, and all my tools have been replaced. Instead of a regular sized shovel, spade or rake, I downsized to hand tools with midsized handles, giving me a two-foot reach. When it doesn't reach without bending, it's time to move. These smaller tools are lighter and much easier on my whole body. You can still overwork, so pay attention to your body. I also reuse plastic grocery bags for weeding. One bag a day limit; must sit on the ground, and no stooping!

I can't remember the last time I actually cleaned the house the way I used to. We invested in a good, lightweight vacuum I can actually use. My problem was over stretching with the vacuum and then pulling it back. Vacuuming is one of the hardest household chores for a woman's body. A doctor taught me that years ago after a hernia surgery. Now, instead of standing in one spot pushing and pulling the vacuum, I walk with my vacuum. Walking alongside the vacuum prevents me from overstretching and helps preserve my back. It's a great tidbit for anyone who vacuums. Next time don't push and pull, take your vacuum for a walk!

Undressing can be very difficult. Most days, I cannot cross my arms in front of me to grab the bottom of my shirt and pull it over my head. On a good day, I can reach my hands behind my head and grab the neck of my shirt to pull it off over my head. On a bad day, I ask Jack to take my shirt off. Sadly, it's not romantic. Bad days have lots of groans, even in a hot shower.

Check your office chair. My office chair has a back that slowly sinks down to the bottom cushion. Remember to check your chair and keep the lumbar support where you need it.

Shoulder pinches seem to be a favorite among physical therapists. It's as simple as it sounds; just pinch your shoulders together feeling the pull between your shoulder blades. Great for posture!

Be more aware of your surroundings. Keep the things you use most often close to you. Rearrange your desk so the phone, the stapler, and the note pad are within easy reach, and make any changes as needed. This really helps. Move things that you rarely use further to the back of the desk. Pay attention and use your best movement when you need something farther away from you. This is also true for the fridge. Put the items you use most often on the most comfortable shelf for your reach.

I am pretty sure this is a side effect of the concussion: When watching TV, I can't always understand what they are saying. I rewind, close my eyes, and play it again. Sometimes I actually hear better when I close my eyes and focus only on what's being said.

Pillows are another best friend! When I lie down, I use pillows to support my body. I am a side sleeper, so I use a pillow to support my top arm, keeping it even with my shoulder. I also like a longer pillow for my knees and feet. I found that if I only have a small pillow between my knees and let my ankles come together, my knees hurt. Now I have a long pillow that keeps the knees and ankles the same distance apart, reducing stress on my knees, hips and lower back. When lying on my back, I use a pillow under my knees which also seems to help soothe and relax the lower back.

Watching TV in bed is frequently frowned upon and yet, some days, it is my only connection to the rest of the world. Arrange your nest of pillows so that you are not straining your neck in any way. Have your head, neck and shoulders aligned as well as you can.

I have learned the sound called "white noise" is very soothing to me and helps me sleep. I was introduced to this sound at Dr. Benson's office. One appointment, when I walked into the exam room there was a sound machine playing the ocean with way too many birds, so I changed the knob, listened to the options and loved white noise. Some think that white noise sounds like static, but for me it puts my brain into relax mode. I found a portable, battery operated sound machine that had white noise at my pharmacy. Check the sounds on each unit and make sure there is one that relaxes you. For me, white noise seems to fill in the holes in my brain where the connectors are off a few hairs.

As per the usual disclaimer, check with your doctor or health practitioner to make sure you are healthy and strong enough before you try any of these moves.

"Every calamity is to be overcome by endurance."

~ Virgil (70 BC – 19 BC)

Chapter 19

The Medical Circus Escalates

It had now been 17 months since the wreck. For two weeks I attempted full-on activities, and it set me back past square one. Dr. Gallo said, "It's time to check in with your MD. You shouldn't be having these drastic setbacks. Take a list of your problems to your doctor. If you want, have her call me; I'll be glad to talk with her."

It had been six months since PT. Life was a roller coaster of good days and bad days. The more I could do, the more I wanted to do. The more I did the more setbacks I had. When I had setbacks, I was in bed for a week and had to work up to square one all over again. Something was still not "fixed." I returned to the MD because Dr. Gallo suggested it. At the MD's office, I always felt treated as if I had never been injured. I never got the impression my MD was even concerned. I would always make a list so I wouldn't forget things. I hoped we would have a discussion about my injuries before she lectured me on cholesterol or something else, which seemed so irrelevant. When I brought up my memory issues, she remarked it was the first she had heard of it.

I handed my MD a complete list of my issues and examples of them…how the accident happened, damages to my car, my initial visit to her, and subsequent other modalities of treatment:

chiropractic, massage, CranioSacral therapy, Physical Therapy and Myofascial Release (all which helped a lot!).

I listed all the difficulties I had with brain issues. I had lost my ability to do math/balance checkbook/use calculator, memory loss; difficulty reading, writing, spelling, formulating sentences, and in general, figuring things out.

I listed all my body issues: the headaches, the back spasms and constant icing, the constantly up and down blood pressure, the inability to find a comfortable sleeping position and…the stress!

I listed all the things I was doing for myself: the nutritional supplements to assist my healing, physical therapy, stretching, Pilates, exercise, and heavy medications, as needed.

Last, but never least, the guy at the insurance company says your records say I was hit by a truck. I was hit by a big white van.

The MD quickly glanced over my list, skeptical that my problems were from the wreck. I asked her to call Dr. Gallo and was surprised that she was willing to call. When she returned, she said, "I will schedule you for an MRI and refer you to a neurologist for the memory problems. As for the pain issues, I am out of options, so I'll be referring you to pain management."

"All pain management does is spinal injections. I won't do those," I said indignantly. I know some people that are really helped by the injections, but pumping steroids into my spine with needles? On purpose? I don't think so! The thought horrified me!

"I am sending you to someone I know for a diagnosis, he's very good."

"So I am just going for a diagnosis?"

"Yes. We will contact the neurologist's office and pain management office, and they will contact you. I want to see you after I receive their reports."

"Okay," I said with a sigh. She flashed me a quick smile and left the room. A brain MRI when I wanted my hips checked? I was confused, and then I chuckled inside. Dr. Gallo had suggested I see a neurologist about eight months after the wreck, and I'd started crying. I didn't want to go because I knew they would drill holes in my head. Silly, I know, but a year ago that's what my brain told me, and I believed. Had Dr. Gallo known me before the wreck, she would have known how far out that was, even for me.

Calls were made and calls came in. Everything was scheduled. The MRI would be the following week, and the neurologist appointment was in three weeks. I was surprised my pain management appointment was two months away. There was probably a reason at the time, but I don't remember.

"If you're going through Hell, Keep Going."
~ Winston Churchill (1874 – 1965)

Chapter 20

The Brain MRI

The MD scheduled my brain MRI. Odd, I wanted one of my hips. When I checked in for the test, I found out they would be using contrast (dye) which meant an IV. I followed the tech into a large room with the MRI machine. "That thing is huge; it looks like a giant doughnut on steroids with a table in the middle." She chuckled. I was so nervous. She could see me shaking and was very kind and patient with me.

"Have a seat. This will be a snap, you'll do fine. Once the IV is in, we can start taking pictures. The table will move you through the tube, or doughnut." She smiled. "It's very loud when it's running. When we are complete with the first series, I will move the table out to inject the dye into your IV. Then you're back in the tube, and we will repeat the series with the contrast, you'll need to keep very still. Any questions?"

"Not really. I will do my best; let's go."

"Alright, lie down with your head toward the doughnut and I'll get your IV started." She was good with a needle. I hate needles. "When the time comes, I will inject the dye through your IV. Here are some earplugs to help with the noise, and I want you to hold this while we are testing." She put a squeeze bulb in my hand. "If you have any problems, squeeze this and I'll come right in. Do your best not to move. Are you ready?"

"I'm here, and I want to know what's wrong, but, at the moment, an MRI of my brain sounds really creepy."

"I assure you, you won't feel a thing."

"How long will it take to get the dye out of my system?"

"It should flush out within twenty-four hours."

Once I had the earplugs in and was settled, she made sure I had the bulb in hand.

"Here we go," she said, and the table moved into position. She went to her booth and I heard her voice, "Okay, do your best to be still; we're starting now."

The inside of the tube started knocking. It was as noisy as a freight train, even with the earplugs. It made loud knocking noises like the sound of a giant piston in need of oil. Knock, knock, knock…Although she assured me I wouldn't feel a thing, I felt it. Perhaps it was because I was sensitive to energy shifts caused by the giant magnets they use.

Finally the machine came to a silence. The table moved out of the tube. I heard her voice, "Are you doing okay?"

"So far, so good."

"Okay, I'm injecting the contrast." I could feel the dye enter my body, it felt thick and sludgy and I got a strange taste in my mouth. "Here we go, are you ready?"

"Ready."

"Okay, hold still." The table slid back into the tube. Once again I heard the loud knocking. When the machine finally stopped, I heard her say, "Okay, you did great. We're finished." When I sat up; I felt lightheaded. She was right there for me. "Lie back down for a minute, honey. Do you feel nauseous?"

"No, just really dizzy." I thought it was the dye but I kept quiet.

"Give yourself a few minutes and then try again." After a few minutes I sat up again.

"Are you doing alright?"

"I'll be fine. I just need to sit a few minutes. I don't want to stand too soon and take the chance of falling over."

"Sounds like a good idea," she said smiling. I took some nice deep breaths and relaxed a bit. When I stood, I was a little wobbly but able to walk. She escorted me back to the lobby, and we said our goodbyes. I was surprised to find an hour had passed.

I left the building and saw Jack driving over to me. I got in the car and home we went. I felt dizzy and woozy for the rest of the day. My back hurt, so I used some ice and took a nap. I woke up with a horrific headache that lasted most of the night. Thankfully, when I woke the next day, my head felt better. I didn't care for that brain MRI. I hope it tells them something.

"To realize that you do not understand is a virtue;
Not to realize that you do not understand is a defect."
~ Lao Tzu (6th Century)

Chapter 21

Neurology

I received paperwork from the neurologist's office; a big packet full of the same questions on different letterhead. My instincts kept tugging at me to change doctors and see the neurologist my chiropractor knew. To my regret, I did not follow those instincts, and the neurologist I went to was not a fan of chiropractic or alternative treatment options.

The day came for my appointment. I was nervous; tightly holding onto my paperwork. Jack drove, and I did my best to ignore traffic. I checked in and handed in my paperwork. As usual there was more to fill out. "Why don't they just send it all at the same time?"

We waited in the lobby and then in the exam room. Finally, the doctor came in and introduced himself. I got on the table and he checked my reflexes. He did a few of those, "don't let me push down, don't let me push up" tests on my arms and legs. I thought it odd he spent less time doing basic neurological checks than my chiropractor did. Next he gave me three words to remember. Then he had me write something on a piece of paper and then he asked me to repeat the three words. The writing only had one misspelled word. It took me a while to remember the three words, but I did remember them.

After his prodding, he sent me on my way for two more tests and blood work. One of the blood tests was for syphilis. I laughed inside. I know it can eat your brain and it's probably good to rule it out, but I laughed because I had to have a syphilis test before I could get into hairdressing school back in the 1980s.

One test was an EEG and the other was a neuropsych exam. Neuropsychology? He thinks I am crazy! What if they locked me up for being crazy? I don't think crazy is against the law yet. So with the doctor visit, two tests, and surely another follow-up visit, that's four more bills. How am I going to pay for these tests? Time to breathe...At times, it's very difficult to let the panic go, even though you know it does you no good. If you didn't know that, you do now. Panic never helps; it only drains your reserves!

The EEG (Electroencephalogram) was done on an out-patient basis at a local hospital. The attendant stuck little electrodes all over my head. Each electrode was attached to a wire to feed my brain waves into a computer. It felt so strange, I had to get up and look in the mirror. I looked hilarious with all those wires sticking out of my head, like a modern day electric Medusa. Even though Jack wasn't allowed in during the actual test, I just had to call Jack to come in. I couldn't deprive him of such a funny sight. I wish I had a picture of it!

Once we had a good laugh, the attendant got serious and explained how the test measured brain activity and records it on the screen so a doctor can read it. Jack was sent away from the room so the test could proceed without distraction. The attendant had me lie down and put a hard round pillow under my neck, carefully adjusting the wires so they were all in their right places. The pillow was like a rock; very uncomfortable, but we couldn't move it because of the electrodes. I lay there staring at the ceiling trying my best to ignore the oncoming spasms in my back. I focused on my breath and counted patterns in the ceiling tiles until I fell asleep. The next thing I knew, the attendant was waking me up. Jack was allowed back in while he detached everything from my head. Then he showed us what my scan looked like.

"It looks pretty normal," he said, pointing out the two different sides of my brain. All I saw were two graphs. I wondered why none of the wonderful technology medical science claims to have could find out what the problem was. We thanked him and headed home. I went to bed with ice and slept the rest of the day.

It's amazing how many doctor bills you get from doctors you have never heard of. One doctor orders the test, one gives the test, one reads the test, and then back to the doctor who ordered the test so they can tell you what the other doctor said. It's an expensive system! Thank goodness we had good health insurance. Without the insurance write off, I can't imagine how people pay the inflated "retail" prices.

I miss the days of good old fashioned family doctors who had diagnostic skills and instincts; they didn't depend on machines. When I was growing up, they would order a test to prove their diagnosis. Now they seem to use tests to rule everything out to make a diagnosis. I hope doctors don't only study "big pharma" medicine. Nowadays, I'd like to think they have classes in energy, nutrition and wellness, and also how to look at, and address the human body as a whole.

Next on the list was the neuropsychology testing. The doctor the neurologist referred me to didn't take insurance and required $2,700 cash, up front. I researched for a week and found another doctor in town who took my insurance, so I made the appointment with her.

Jack and I drove downtown to meet Dr. Rogers. She specialized in neuropsychology and rehabilitation for head injuries. I hoped she would be able to find out what was going on with my brain. We signed in at the reception desk, sat down, and waited.

After a few minutes, my name was called. The office was very comfortable. We all sat at a round table, and she began asking all kinds of questions. "What problems are you having? How did you do in school? How did you get along with your parents?" The questions went on and on.

"I know something is wrong, but no one has figured it out."

"It's a good sign you know there's a problem. When people don't know there's a problem, then it's *really* a problem."

She took the time to explain the test and the different stages. It would be a timed test administered by her assistant and could take up to five hours. My heart sank; I thought we would be testing today. Dr. Rogers spent about 45 minutes with us, asking and answering questions, explaining everything. I felt like she really cared and thought I found someone who would help me. She walked us out of her office and back to the lobby and we set the appointment for the actual test.

A week later I drove myself to the test. I didn't want Jack to sit around waiting for five hours. At the office, my heart felt like it would jump out of my chest. I was afraid of how long it would take to bounce back from this test. Within minutes my name was called, and I was taken back to an office. Dr. Rogers' assistant was behind her desk and all business. She got up, introduced herself, and we got started.

"Today's test is a timed test. A certain amount of time is allotted for each section. We will be moving quickly." The testing began. I was tested with cards and pictures, quizzed on math, logic, and mechanical thinking. She took notes as I worked on each section. The minute we finished one test, we would move right on to the next one. It was exhausting. Fortunately we came to a test now and then when I could stand and stretch because I didn't have to look at anything directly. Tears were rolling down my cheeks. My body was starting to seize up. I was more miserable by the minute. All the thinking made my head throb. We have to figure out what's going on in here.

My tester was becoming impatient. After only two hours, she started watching the clock. She set me up for the next test using the computer. Once I had started, she left the room and came back with her coffee. An hour later, I asked to go to the bathroom.

"This is a timed test."

"I have to go to the bathroom. We are in between sections."

With a huff, she gave me directions to the bathroom. All the tests moved so fast my head was spinning. It was nice to have a minute alone in the bathroom just to breathe. I rinsed my face with cold water. I went back and sat down. She was all set up for the next test. I was told this test might last five hours so I thought we were scheduled until 6:00. She kept glancing at her watch. At 4:30 she informed me she would have to leave soon to catch her bus. She kept an eye on her clock and began packing her things.

"The rest of the testing is on the computer. I will get you started, and then I need to catch my bus. When you are finished, hit this button to close your test. There will be someone at the window; let them know you are done, and then you can leave."

I felt abandoned. I was prepared for a five hour test; why wasn't she? It made me feel slow and stupid. Finally I finished and hit the exit key. I let them know at the window I was finished. I was so thankful it was over. It was awful. I was panicky just thinking about the drive home in rush hour traffic. I left the building and hobbled down the sidewalk into the parking garage. I sat in my car and cried. After a few minutes, I turned on my cell phone, and called Jack. I needed to hear his voice.

When Jack answered, I started crying again.

"How was it?" he said calmly.

"It was awful, everything hurts. I have one of those thinking headaches and it's really bad. That test was awful! My head is doing that bowling ball thing." Jack listened patiently as I blurted everything out through tears.

"I feel a little better now; hearing your voice always helps."

"Let's talk some more, you don't have to drive right now."

"I had no idea how bad this test would be. I'll be down icing for days." After talking with Jack, I was much calmer. I wanted to be home but I was in no shape to drive. We kept talking until the clock was pushing 6:00.

"Well Jack, I better get on the road."

"I love you, take your time coming home, and be careful."

"I love you too. We've talked so long most of the traffic will have cleared. I promise I'll be careful and take my time."

"Okay honey, be careful, I will see you soon." I listened as he hung up the phone.

I wouldn't wish that test on anyone. It was really, really bad. My head was still pounding. I took nice deep breaths preparing to drive. I kept telling myself everything was fine. I pulled out into traffic. My heart pounded harder as I pulled onto the highway. I only lasted a few miles before I had to get away from all those drivers. I took an exit and cut through town. It was a longer drive, but easier on me.

When I got home, Jack was waiting for me with a gentle hug. He still worried about hurting me when he hugged me. We both did. I took two pain pills and laid down on ice packs for twenty minutes and then took a hot shower. That's homemade Hydrotherapy. I got out of the shower and put on my bathrobe. I blew a kiss to Jack and slowly climbed the stairs to bed.

We returned to Dr. Rogers' office a week later for the neuropsychology follow-up and test results. She handed me a copy as we sat down. According to their assessment, I was okay but had "mild depression." Good news and bad; that meant no brain answers here.

Dr. Rogers suggested a speech therapist for my stutter. It's not actually a stutter, it's Scrabble® mouth. My brain gets flashes and what comes out of my mouth is not what I'm seeing in my head. I say words and make them connect until I get the word I'm looking for. She told me to go easy on myself when this happens; take a breath and start over.

She also recommended that I use a date book for the memory issue, writing down my schedule for keeping track of the days, which I was already doing. Her last recommendation was to work on my sleep hygiene, meaning going to bed and getting up at the same time every day, which is hard to do when pain runs your schedule.

Once again she told me, "Since you know there's a problem, that's a good sign. People with truly severe brain injuries oftentimes are not aware of what they are doing. So the fact that you know that there is a problem, the fact you are aware of the problem, is a very good sign."

"My brain feels like all the circuits are off just a hair and aren't connecting correctly. Is it possible my brain has micro-tears from bouncing around in there?"

"I suppose that's possible..." I could see her thinking about it. Maybe she had never been asked that before. You get micro-tears in your neck muscles from whiplash; it's not a stretch to believe that my brain had tears too.

"I will fax your report to the neurologist today. If I can be of further assistance, please call."

"Thank you." She walked out to the lobby with us.

Now that we had gone over the test results with Dr. Rogers, it was time to return to the neurologist.

I made my neurology follow-up appointment. The doctor had the results of the EEG but said he hadn't received a copy of the neuropsychology report. All this waiting and he didn't have all the test results? I was angry. He didn't even seem concerned that he didn't have the results. The EEG looked fine, so he was not concerned about my brain. I was confused. I thought a neurologist would check the whole nervous system, but he said I was there so he could check out my brain and that was all. That really confused me because I knew my nervous system was much more than my brain. And he's a neurologist, not a brainologist. I remember his last words to me, "I won't waste anymore of your money." That made me very angry...did he think I was making it all up? No way man; this is too hard.

At least he asked what Dr. Rogers had told me. I said, "She says that knowing I have a problem is a good sign."

"She is right about that," he agreed.

When we left his office, Jack drove straight to the rehab center where I had taken the neuropsychology test. The man at the front desk made a call, put the receiver down, and said, "Dr. Rogers will be out in a moment."

Before I sat down, I saw Dr. Rogers was coming down the hall. "Come on back, what can I do for you?" She said with a smile.

"The neurologist said he didn't have your results back yet."

She looked perplexed. "I know I faxed those." I followed her like a puppy as she went to get the file. She opened the folder. My results were sitting on top, stamped "faxed" and dated. "This was sent over a week ago," she said with a sigh. "Usually someone other than the doctor gets the fax and files it before the doctor ever sees it."

She had the open folder in one hand, feeding the fax machine with the other. I heard a slight snarl in her voice as she mumbled, "This is the second time I've sent this report. I know they already have this." I heard her breathe and her voice relaxed. She had surrendered. "Well, now we can both be sure they were sent." I watched as the pages were sucked into the machine, and a confirmation sheet followed. She walked me to the lobby and I said, "Thank you so much."

Jack was outside in the car waiting for me. I told him, "She sent the report again, and the original fax was dated over a week ago. She didn't seem too happy with the neurologist's office." I saw no point in returning to the neurologist for his take on the report now. I wouldn't want to waste any more of his time. Dr. Rogers had gone over the report with Jack and me. I had little doubt that she explained the results better than the neurologist could have. So what's the point of going back to him again? I knew I should have changed doctors and gone to the neurologist my chiropractor suggested. There's that 20/20 hindsight again.

"The greatest evil is physical pain."

~ Saint Augustine (354 – 430)

Chapter 22

Pain Management

I received the packet from the pain management clinic. It was pages and pages and pages. I was instructed to fill them out and bring them with me to my appointment. The page that had the body diagram that said, "Tell us what hurts" had markings all over it. I could have circled the whole picture and been honest.

The clinic was located in a local hospital. When we checked in at the reception desk, we were politely told to have a seat. We waited for two hours. My body was throbbing when we were finally called. The nurse said Jack couldn't go in with me. I said, "I want him with me."

"He can come back later after we get you settled in." I followed her through the door and into a room. She asked if there were any abuse issues at home. I chuckled at the thought, shook my head and said, "No."

She said "we have to ask."

"I understand, I do, it's okay. But not my Jack; never!"

"Alright, your husband can come back now."

Jack quietly appeared in the doorway. I looked at him and

smiled. The nurse pointed to a chair, and he sat down. She asked for my films.

"I don't have any films."

"That's unusual; most patients have had MRIs before they come to us."

"My MD sent me here for a diagnosis. I'm not here for a spinal injection."

"Injections are all we do here," she said matter of factly.

"My doctor sent me here for a diagnosis, not for injections. I want to know what's wrong." I kept looking at Jack to stay strong about the injections.

She looked surprised for a moment and then let it go. She took my blood pressure; "150/90, that's about right."

It's interesting what the blood pressure range is for different doctors. At 130/90, the chiropractor asked if I was in pain. At 130/85, my MD gave me a lecture about how 120/80 is considered normal and wanted me on pills immediately. At 150/90, the pain management clinic nurse said, "That's about right. Blood pressure tends to be higher when you're in pain," then handed me a gown and said, "Leave it open in the back; the doctor will be in soon."

Another two hours and we finally caught a glimpse of the doctor. He stuck his head in the door and apologized for running so late and said he would be right back. After another half hour, he finally returned with time to see me. He too, was unaware I had no films.

"So your injuries are from a motor vehicle accident?"

"Yes, I was broadsided and spun in circles."

"When was that?" he inquired.

"About a year and a half ago."

"So this is already settled then?"

"No."

For a moment he looked like a deer in the headlights. I watched him turn pale as the blood drained from his face. He looked down and started flipping through paperwork. He asked questions, I told him where it hurt. He poked and prodded, stretched me and flexed me. My body was already throbbing from the five-hour wait and all his testing triggered muscle spasms. I was blinking away tears, trying to tough it out. My doctor's name was paged over the loudspeaker. "I'll be back," and he vanished.

I was exhausted from sitting and my head was a bowling ball. The pain was ten times worse than when we arrived hours ago. The tears came. Jack handed me some tissues and stroked my head. Jack knew I had been up too long and was really hurting. I was in that weepy, vulnerable place. We were both way past impatient. Jack said, "Why don't you lie down? There's no telling when he'll get back."

"That sounds like a great idea," I groaned a few times trying to find a comfortable position on the exam table. Another half hour had gone by. Jack was standing in the doorway, watching and waiting for the doctor.

"This is bullshit!" I knew Jack wasn't happy.

"I agree." I wasn't happy either, but I was doing better since lying down.

The doctor finally returned full of apologies and finished his poking and prodding. "I have my suspicions, but since you don't have films, I am sending you for a cervical and a lumbar MRI so we can see what's going on in there."

Since it was a pain management clinic, I asked for pain meds. Guess that's the junkie question. The doctor turned harsh and indignant. Perhaps he was insulted I wouldn't do the spinal injections. "Do you just want me to give you the name of a doctor that hands out pills?"

"No," I whimpered, "I am in pain and I want to know what's wrong. The longer I'm here, the worse I feel, and after all your poking and prodding, I'll be in bed with ice for a week." I was crying again. I was in a pain management clinic. I needed help and he was angry with me?

The doctor sized me up and softened a bit. "I tell you what; I will give you a prescription for some pain meds so you don't end up in the ER some night with back spasms. The nurse will be in shortly to schedule your MRIs and a follow up visit." Again he vanished. Jack had me dressed before the nurse came back with the paperwork.

"Here is the information for your MRI appointment, now let's get you scheduled for your follow-up, and we'll see you at your next visit." She handed me an appointment card for my follow-up, then pointed us toward the exit.

I thanked her and politely said, "See you soon."

Jack drove me to the diagnostic center for my MRIs. I figured the neck and lower back MRIs had to be better than the brain MRI, plus no dye this time which meant no IV. I went dressed for the occasion and got right in. I had to lay back and relax and let the machine do its work.

The table was prepared for my MRIs. I wasn't as nervous since I knew what to expect. I laid down on the table, and I was handed my earplugs. When I was settled into place, the table moved into the tube. Doing both areas took just over an hour. I felt like I was stuck forever inside a knocking train. The machine quit knocking and I was retrieved from the tube.

"I'll get these to the radiologist, he'll fill out his report, and you'll be ready to go back to your doctor," she said with a wink.

When the day came to revisit the pain management center, we signed in and waited. This wait was not as long as the last visit. We were called within an hour and escorted to the exam room where the doctor was actually waiting for us. He had the films on the X-ray board. He disagreed with the original report. He showed us areas in the neck where there were bulging discs and another spot in the lower back with more bulging. He smiled and said cheerfully, "The good news is you don't have any spinal tumors." That certainly was good news.

The pain management clinic mainly utilized spinal injections. He explained how the injections worked. First, you were sedated and then they take a picture so they know, in real-time, where to aim the needle. If the shot didn't help within a week or two, they did another shot in another spot. The maximum was three treatments.

I told him I understood how it worked but I wasn't interested. I came for a diagnosis. They also perform nerve oblation. That's when the nerve is clipped so there are no more pain signals. That didn't sound smart either. The pain was from something. Making it go away by clipping the nerve wouldn't solve the problem underneath the pain.

The doctor suggested more physical therapy and sent me back to the MD. I left the clinic feeling confused. Last time the doctor barked at me when I asked for pain medication that cost a few bucks but he was happy to do spinal injections that cost $500? The injections are covered by insurance, in case you were curious. Until I knew exactly what was wrong, I was not going to let them pump steroids into my spine, and Jack backed up my decision.

"We shall draw from the heart of suffering itself
the means of inspiration and survival."
~Winston Churchill (1874 — 1965)

Chapter 23

MD Follow-up

I had been to the neurologist and the pain management clinic and taken their tests. Now it was time to return to my MD's office. When I called to schedule my follow-up appointment, I asked if all the test results were back and was told, "Yes they had them, but the soonest they could see me was in two weeks."

My blood pressure was a bit high at my first visit after the wreck, and she wanted me on blood pressure medication. She never considered pain as the cause or the fact that I have severe white-coat syndrome. She gave me a lecture on blood pressure, heart attacks, and strokes and how it could all happen to me because my blood pressure was so high. It was only 130 over something and she freaked me out for a week. I was afraid my own anxiety and panic would cause a heart attack. Jack went to the drugstore and bought a blood pressure monitor so I could monitor my blood pressure at home; smart guy. I charted my blood pressure for two months and brought my BP sheets to my next appointment so they could be added to my file.

I was so stressed about seeing the MD again, I got very little sleep. It seems I always got a lecture from her which only increased my white-coat syndrome.

When the day came, Jack drove. We sat in the waiting room until our name was called. She followed the recommendation from pain management and scheduled me for three more weeks of physical therapy. The MD seemed very nonchalant about it all, and was more concerned about my cholesterol levels. Enough with the cholesterol already; how do I find out what is wrong with me?

I felt I had done all I could do, staying true to myself, and trying to please her. I'd seen her doctors and taken their tests and, still, no one could agree on what was wrong with me. I will do more physical therapy and keep going to my chiropractor; at least I feel better when I do that.

"Some single mind must be master, else there will be no agreement in anything."
~ Abraham Lincoln (1809 – 1865)

Chapter 24

When the Doctors Don't Agree, It's Time for an I.M.E.

It had been over a year and a half since the wreck. I was still in pain, still frustrated and still without answers. I slowly taught myself to read and write uppercase and lower case letters, print and cursive. When I had those mastered, two inches high, I practiced writing smaller. I still had horrible headaches and crippling body pain. I'd been through rounds of physical therapy, seen specialists, and been through medical testing from hell. I felt attacked by the other driver's insurance company and all but dismissed by my own. My best friends were now ice packs and heating pads.

Dr. Sebastian was concerned. "We have been working with you for a long time. I know something isn't right or you wouldn't relapse so easily and so often." There was definitely something wrong no one had found yet, and we both knew it.

"Even living at half-speed, it's still like two steps forward and four steps back, and then I have to start all over again to work back up to square one." I could feel the tears coming. "This has to stop before I go mad! The worst thing is that I'll do something and I don't hurt for hours. I don't get the delayed pain thing. If

165

it hurt while I was doing something, I would know to stop, but the pain gives me no warning."

"I think we should send you for an I.M.E."

"What is that?" I asked with great apprehension.

"It is an Independent Medical Exam. One doctor gets all your available medical records and performs a physical exam. He goes through everything, and I mean everything. Hopefully he will find some answers. It's about time to get you medically released, but I can't release you until we know more." I was desperate for answers but this sounded like another exam from hell.

"Have you ever heard of Dr. Benson?"

"No, who is he?"

"He's an osteopath and orthopedic man. I met him at a conference where he was lecturing. He seems very good at what he does. You can't go to a doctor you have seen before for this exam. So, if you know him, please let me know and we will find someone else."

"No problem, I've never heard of him."

"Understand, it will take time for him to get all your records. Be patient a little longer. I really think he can help."

"Okay," I sighed and took his card.

"I was impressed with him, and I think he can figure things out." She had always pegged it right so far, and I had no reason to doubt her on this. I was so tired, the pain was so exhausting. I needed answers!

I called Dr. Benson's office to make my appointment for the I.M.E.

The first question was, "Have you ever seen Dr. Benson before?"

"No."

"Good, if you had, he wouldn't qualify to do your exam. What are your injuries?"

"I was in a car wreck almost two years ago and there's still something wrong."

She took some basic information and said, "I will mail you a packet. There will be a questionnaire and medical history for you to fill out and we will need a list of all the doctors you have ever been to, along with a medical release so we can request records from all the doctors."

"I have medical records I can bring in."

"We can start there but we need to request and receive your records directly from your doctors. The exam fee is $600 and payment is required before your exam."

"You also need to know that insurance will not pay for independent exams. Do you have a lawyer we need to contact?"

"No."

"The packet will also include a schedule of the doctor's other fees and services, should there be a trial. May I ask who referred you to us?"

"Dr. Sebastian, my chiropractor; she also does sports medicine. She met Dr. Benson at a conference."

"Thank you. I will get your packet in the mail today."

"Thank you," I replied. I felt that gripping feeling of overwhelm as I hung up the phone. $600 up front? After two years, my cash reserves were tapped out. Once I stopped crying, I called Mom with the update. She said not to worry; she'd cover the $600 so I could get on with the next step. Thank God for the Bank of Mom.

I received the packet. It took days to fill out, and then I made a copy for me. My back was already hurting and my right side was cramping even before the copies were started. Then off I went to the other side of town to drop off all the paperwork along with a check to Dr. Benson's office.

There was so much traffic, and I was really scared. Seeing other drivers horrified me. I couldn't trust any of them. I felt my whole body tighten up. My neck felt like it shrunk an inch. It was a long morning; I was only out a couple of hours but, man, I was hurting and exhausted. I really looked forward to lying down with ice when I got home.

One week later, Jack and I arrived for the exam and I checked in at the front desk. I waited anxiously until I heard my name called.

"Hi, I'm Carol. I'll be assisting Dr. Benson today for your exam." She showed us into a large room. We sat in chairs and she sat at the end of the exam table with paperwork in front of her.

"First thing we will do today for the exam is a complete medical history on you." She began asking all kinds of questions and writing notes. It felt like an inquisition; on and on and on it went. I kept thinking, "You already have all this information so why do I have to answer it again? The answers are always the same." I assumed she was asking questions and taking notes so they had the information straight from the horse's mouth, so to speak. The intake interview took hours. I could feel myself already drooping.

When she was done asking questions and straightening her notes, she laid out a gown for me. She stood up and said, "Go ahead and get changed the doctor will be with you shortly." She collected her papers and left the room, closing the door behind her. Jack helped me undress and get into the gown.

Soon, there was a knock on the door and Dr. Benson and Carol entered the room. Carol took her seat at the end of the table. The doctor explained, "The I.M.E. is an Independent Medical Exam, and independent means independent, period. Insurance never covers the exam because then I could be accused of bias. I don't work for you, the insurance company, or anybody else. It's my job to give a neutral, honest assessment of your condition. I am an advocate for the medical record. If I have not pleased anybody, I have done my job. My evaluation will be based on the exam we're doing today and all your medical records. I want to see everything from every doctor you have ever seen. If you had previous accidents or previous injuries, I want to know about them. I want everything from any doctor you can remember. Once my report is complete, I can treat you or you can take the results somewhere else for treatment."

He paused for a moment. I could see him thinking. "You need to understand, if I complete my report and your case goes to court and someone presents me with a medical report I have never seen before, my report would then be incomplete. I would need to incorporate that medical report with the report I already prepared to continue testifying. We have requested all your records and have a few in so far. I prefer to do the exam first before looking at any of your records. That way, I form my own opinion first and then I examine your records."

His manner felt cold when he spoke, and he didn't make much

eye contact. I guess that's how he stays neutral. "Let's get started shall we? I will be talking and Carol will take down the information. We will be moving quickly."

He had brought in a black box full of exam tools. I soon came to call this "the black box of torture." It was full of instruments to measure all kinds of responses. One looked like an old fashioned tracing wheel for sewing. He rolled it down both arms. I couldn't feel anything as it rolled down my right forearm, or my ring and little fingers. Carol wrote notes as he rattled off medical jargon.

He used a hinged plastic ruler to measure how far I could turn my head to either side and backwards and forwards. He measured my movement bending sideways at the waist. He kept measuring and rattling off numbers, and she kept taking notes. Then, the, "don't let me push your hands down, don't let me push your hands up" started. He did the same tests with my feet; "don't let me push your feet down, don't let me push your feet up." I was already worn out, and we were barely into the exam. The tests continued as he poked, and he spoke while Carol wrote. After five hours, it was finally over. We scheduled the appointment to come back for his preliminary findings.

My body was racked with pain, and my brain was on overload. I wanted to be home, and I was so thankful Jack was driving.

"How are you doing?" Jack asked when we got outside.

"Awful," I said with a gasp, "but I brought my meds. I figured this test would really suck. I didn't want to take any before so he could see how I am without medication."

I was so glad to be outside feeling the sun. Jack opened the door for me. "We'll be home soon honey, hang on. I think it's time for an ice pack, don't you?"

My voice quivered as I whined, "Just get me home please." I downed a couple of pain pills. It was a quiet ride home. My head was a bowling ball, and I really needed to rest. I knew it was hard for Jack, too, seeing me in that kind of pain. Sad, the two of us in the same car, both hurting, loving each other and, in that moment, there was nothing we could do for each other.

Pain steals your life away. Whether it's the pain of the patient, or the pain of the caretakers who love them and can't fix them; pain steals life.

When we pulled in the driveway, I was so glad to be home! Jack helped me out of the car and into the house. The pain was so bad I could barely stand up. "You head upstairs and I'll bring up your ice." I slowly crawled up the stairs on my hands and knees and got onto the bed. The pain kept getting worse, so I took another pain pill.

I could barely move my arms, I couldn't bend over and I couldn't sit. I said, "My bender and my sitter are broke." Jack got my clothes off and helped me settle into bed, tucking pillows in all the right places. One pillow for my head, two pillows for my back, and one more from my knees to my feet to help prevent lower back pain, another pillow to rest my top arm on to square my chest and help keep pressure off my rib and tension out of my top shoulder. Then he gently wedged an ice pack between my lower back and the pillows behind me. The other ice pack went under my neck. He kissed me on the forehead, looked into my eyes and softly said, "I love you."

I smiled softly, "I'm glad."

"You rest, honey. I'll be back up after a while." He came back soon after to check on me and retrieve the ice bags.

"How are you feeling?"

"Miserable and whiny, I'm cold! Everything hurts and the pills aren't working."

"Try to relax, okay? I'll bring you some more ice later."

"Okay…thank you for taking care of me. I love you, Jack."

"I love you too, honey." He gave me a gentle kiss on the forehead and went downstairs. I think the hardest part for Jack was that he couldn't fix me, and he hated seeing me in so much pain for so long. I snuggled under the covers and waited for the pain to stop. It never did. Finally, gratefully, I slept out of sheer exhaustion.

My routine of chiropractic and tissue work continued. I was impatient waiting to know the results of the I.M.E. There had to be an answer.

We returned to Dr. Benson's office weeks later. He explained his report was only preliminary because he was still missing records from two doctors. The report was filled with fancy words but, essentially, it confirmed I wasn't faking. I was suffering from chronic post-traumatic neck and shoulder pain consistent with whiplash, post-traumatic stress disorder, and post-traumatic anxiety disorder. My right arm and lower back may have impinged nerves. There was a sternocostal mass (referring to the swollen cartilage between my rib and my breastbone), and bursitis of both greater outer trochanters (the head of the thigh bone). His opinion, pending review of all the medical records, was that I was "not at maximum medical improvement for injuries sustained." He said, "You're whole nervous system is inflamed. "That explained a lot. I wondered why the neurologist didn't catch that. "With this preliminary report done, I can treat you or I can send you to someone else." I didn't need to think about it, "I'll stick with you for treatment."

"Well…Your X-rays are two years old, so let's get new X-rays of the neck and lower back. We can do those here or you can go to the hospital for them. I want a CT scan of that rib and I'm also sending you to a pain management clinic for an EMG."

My guts jumped. "Pain management?" I yelped.

"It's okay; don't worry. I only use this one clinic and this one doctor for this specific test called Electromyography, better known as an EMG. It checks neural pathway connections. We'll get you scheduled for the tests. I'll see you back here in two weeks."

At least with his preliminary report done and with a diagnosis, my health insurance would cover the tests. They already had a lien on my settlement to make sure they got their money back. The doctor also gave me restrictions. "No overhead work, no pushing or pulling, no lifting, and no repetitive grasping."

I chuckled and said, "I know, if it hurts don't do it."

"Yes, that's exactly right" he said with a grin.

"That's what Mom says."

"See, you're paying me for a second opinion." We all chuckled.

His office was set up to do X-rays, so we scheduled an appointment. I arrived the next week and Carol led me to the X-ray room. "We will be doing a neck series, the rib, and the lower back. We'll start with the neck first, then the rib, and then I'll have you lie down on that machine for the back X-rays. Okay?"

"Okay, let's get them done."

Carol placed me standing up against an X-ray machine on the wall. She would position me and say, "inhale and hold," and then snap the picture. The positions were specific and painful. She needed one shot with my mouth wide open. I didn't open wide enough so she pulled my lower jaw down even more, instantly summoning tears to my eyes.

"That hurt!" flew out of my mouth.

"I'm so sorry. I didn't mean to be so rough," she said with genuine concern. "Can you hang in there for me?"

"Just get it done." I felt the headache creeping up the right side of my neck and across my ear, heading for my cheek and eye. She snapped the picture and the standing part was done.

Next she had me lie down on my side on the X-ray table for the lower back pictures. I had to bring my knees up and round my back, like the fetal position. She saw the tears rolling down my cheeks and said, "I will be as gentle as I can, but the doctor needs these specific X-rays, okay? Can you hang in there with me?" I signaled with a shake of my head afraid that if I spoke, I would start crying from the pain and never stop.

Saving the worst for last, next I had to bring my knees up even higher, inciting excruciating pain. When she was done, she told me to relax while she checked to make sure all the films were good. The cramping in my back turned into full-fledged spasms. I wobbled over to the tissue box and blew my nose and wiped my face. She soon returned saying the X-rays were fine, and she had all she needed. I was so ready to go home and hide under the covers with my ice. I felt ashamed for being such a wimp. They were only X-rays, but moving into those positions stirred everything up again and my body was screaming for mercy. I am tired of hurting more after an appointment than before. Jack and I had a few errands planned, but I felt so dreadful, he took me home first, tucked me in, and he did the errands later.

Jack drove me to the pain clinic for the EMG Dr. Benson ordered. I didn't know what to expect; my anxiety just kept rising. When we got there, we were greeted by a friendly nurse. Coming from behind her I saw a familiar face.

Kay looked at the other nurse with a smirk and said, "I'll take this one."

"Hi Kay, I didn't know you were working here."

"Have a seat kids; I'll be right back. I'm going to get you both some water."

I had known Kay for years. I always appreciated her dry wit. Just knowing she was there helped calm me down. She returned with our water. "So, Wendy, what brings you here?"

"I'm having an EMG; still car-wreck testing after two years." She knew me well enough to hear how nervous I was.

"Calm down, you're in good hands. I checked your chart and the doctor doing your test is one of the best. Are you familiar with the EMG?"

"Nope."

"It's not too bad."

"Yeah, right, I've heard that one before!" I said sarcastically.

"Now Wendy, listen to me." She paused until she had my full attention. In a slow, calm voice she said, "Listen to me. The doctor will use two needle electrodes to check the circuitry of your nervous system."

I grinned, popped my eyebrows, and said, "Uh-huh."

"In simple terms, the electrodes are placed on each end of the nerve to see if it's communicating. You can also observe how the muscles are responding."

A groan flew out of one of the cubicles. "I need to check on him. Just breathe and stay calm. Drink your water, and I'll be right back."

When she came back, she asked what had been happening, so I caught her up on everything after the wreck.

"There's your doctor," she said, nodding her head towards the other end of the hall. He came over and introduced himself and told Kay my cubicle number. She made sure the doctor had everything he needed. She looked at me and with a smile said, "See you after, Wendy. Relax, it'll be fine."

The doctor came in and started by explaining the instruments he would be using. They looked like really small knitting needles.

"These run current. I place them in different areas to see how your body responds. I'll start with your forearm so you can see what I am doing."

He placed one needle near my elbow and the other by my wrist, he sent the current through, and my arm jumped involuntarily. It was bizarre. He continued with my arms and then my legs. I felt like a frog in a science class.

It was more weird than painful. A few areas hurt, but not enough to slap him. I told him I was going to write a book.

"Really?" he grinned, as if he had heard that one before.

"Yes! No one knows what happens after a wreck. I used to blame doctors; now I blame insurance companies. Then again, doctors did make the deals with the insurance companies."

"You're right," he said nodding his head. "Insurance companies are a problem, and we doctors bought into it. Hope is good; people need a book like that." He paused for a moment to check his notes. "Okay, let's get you turned over so I can do some checks on your back."

He tested a few places that weren't too bad, but then he tested some points between my shoulder blades, and a scream hurled out of me as I scrambled up the wall to get away from him. "That really hurt!" I shrieked.

"I have never seen that response before."

"That really, really hurt!" I cried. "What does that mean?"

"I will have to look at all the data before giving you any answers. I should have these results to Dr. Benson within the week. You did a really good job; now go home and get some rest, and good luck on your book." We shook hands and he disappeared to the other side of the curtain.

When we came out, Kay asked, "Well, how did you do?"

"He hit two spots on my back that really hurt. Other than that, I think I did okay. I'm exhausted. That's a frog test, man!"

Kay laughed, "I am so glad you still have your sense of humor. It makes all the difference in the world."

"It was a frog test, stick a needle here and stick a needle there and watch the body parts flop around. Weird test! Actually quite tiring, and he wouldn't tell me anything, so I won't know anything until I go back to my doctor. All that's left now is a CT scan of my rib bump." She got a strange look on her face, so I showed it to her.

"Most likely cartilage isn't it?" she asked.

"That's the theory. It hasn't gone down since the wreck, and that was about two years ago. When it flares up, it really hurts. Well lady, it's always a grand time seeing you."

"Too bad we aren't meeting for lunch instead of being stuck in this place!"

"Here, here!" I rang back in agreement. We hugged and she gave Jack a nod. We were out of there and back in the car driving home from yet another test. The place in my back that made me scream was still angry. "I'll be using ice when we get home."

"Thought so," Jack said smiling, as he turned onto the highway. I closed my eyes to ignore the other cars.

All that was left was the CT scan of my rib. I knew a CT scan was something like an MRI but wasn't sure how it actually worked. I showed up in loose clothing with no metal and ready to go, then signed in and waited.

It wasn't long until I heard my name called. I got up and joined the technician in the hall. She showed me to a dressing room, explained how the gown worked, and to make sure it opened toward the front. I told her I wore easy off clothes and it wouldn't take me long. When she returned a few minutes later, I was changed and ready to go.

She took me to a large room with a giant machine that looked like a doughnut with a bed through the middle. It looked a lot like the MRI machine. She explained that "CT stands for Computed

Tomography. A CT scan is a specialized kind of X-ray that takes pictures of cross-section images. Are you ready?"

"Yes, let's do it. It's cold in here."

She had me lie down on the table and asked me to show her the problem rib. I opened up the right side of the gown and showed her the big bump. She said, "I am going to place four patches on you. They're very small and have a little BB in the middle. These line up the shot for the Dr. so he knows he is looking at that particular spot. "She placed two patches on top and two on the bottom. When she had them lined up she said, "We're ready."

"Okay," I said.

"The machine is a bit loud. If you need something, let me know. I can hear you through an intercom." I nodded that I was ready, and she went to the control room outside. I heard her voice coming through the speakers for a sound check. I responded and off we went.

The table moved through the tube until my chest was in the middle. I heard her say, "We're going to start, so don't move." Then the machine started spinning around and taking pictures. The test itself only took about ten minutes—much faster than the MRIs. She came back into the room and helped me sit up. I was lightheaded, so I sat for a few minutes before I stood up. She told me that the doctor would probably have the report within a week. I thanked her as she walked me back to the dressing room.

This was much easier than the EMG, although I was still exhausted from pain, worry, and lack of sleep. When we got home, Jack helped me get undressed. He saw the little BB patches and asked what they were. I explained as I got ready for a steamy shower and then it was off to bed. All the tests were done. I slept.

I called Dr. Benson's office to see if the missing medical records had showed up, which they had, so he finally had everything he needed. We set my follow-up appointment for two weeks out so he had time to complete his final report.

It was time to go in for the results. We arrived at Dr. Benson's office, and without looking up, the lady at the reception desk said, "We will be with you shortly."

The wait seemed like forever; the doctor was way behind schedule. Finally my name was called. We walked back to an exam room and were told the doctor would be in soon. Another hour and finally there was a knock. Dr. Benson walked in with his arms full of files, which he put on the end of the exam table. My heart was pounding! What did he find? What will I be labeled as now?

All the test results were in and Dr. Benson didn't change his recommendations. His final report was as complete as it could be.

It was almost two years after the wreck when Dr. Sebastian referred me to Dr. Benson. It took four months of X-rays, tests, and a pile of medical records before he completed his independent report, which confirmed that my body was really screwed up.

His first recommended treatment was twelve days of steroids to reduce inflammation throughout my whole body, especially the nervous system. Dr. Benson also gave me something to help me sleep. It's very hard to sleep when your back knots up and feels like it was snapped in half, and muscle spasms keep running like waves through your body.

Lack of sleep can be very unhealthy, especially when it's pain related. When you can't sleep, you can't heal. When you can't sleep, you get cranky. When you are cranky, it directly impacts your caretaker. For all you caretakers out there, make sure your "patients" are getting the sleep they need, which will help them heal.

When the round of steroids was complete, I returned to his office. The steroids helped immensely; the inflammation throughout my whole body had diminished. This visit, he started me on a non-steroidal anti-inflammatory, and I was to return in thirty days for another evaluation.

I took the new pills with food and they messed with my stomach. I changed the time so that I was taking the second pill earlier in the day, and that didn't help. After the first week, we had to add another medication, because the new anti-inflammatory drug was giving me horrendous heartburn. Getting sleep was hard enough with the pain, but being awakened by heartburn in the wee hours? That's not right.

Between the sleeping meds and the heartburn meds, I was finally sleeping almost four hours at a stretch. Before starting the meds, I would only sleep for about two hours tops before the pain woke me.

It was time to see Dr. Benson again. By this time, I had been in his care for around six months. More than likely, this would be my last appointment. I knew it was about time for me to be medically released. I felt almost human, and I was finally getting some sleep.

I knew there really wasn't much else medicine could do for my physical body. I knew the drill. Carol would come in and ask questions about how I was doing, and take notes. Then she would get up, head for the door and politely say, "I'll go get the doctor; he'll be in soon."

There would be a knock on the door, and then Dr. Benson would come in with his "little black box of torture." He would poke around and check the spots on the side of my hips where my seatbelt grabbed me. There is no telling how long I had the bursitis before he figured it out. When the bursitis flared up in my hips, he would find the spot the first or second time; my knees would buckle, and he knew it really hurt.

"So why did I get bursitis on my hips like this?"

"It's very common in accidents. The lap belt pulls so tight it irritates those little bursa sacs."

"I had no idea."

"It's really common. Many doctors don't know what to look for. I am more familiar with specific injuries from motor vehicle accidents from doing so many of these exams, plus I see all your records and none of your other doctors have all this information."

He continued to check my upper back and shoulders, looking for signs of inflammation and bursitis. He checked for tingling or numbness in the right arm with that instrument that looks like a tracing wheel. He sat down and wrote some notes.

Then he said, "You certainly look better than the first time I saw you."

"I feel a lot better since we met. Thank you for that. I'm not the person I was before the wreck and may never be, but I feel better."

Dr. Benson closed my gigantic file and said "I can tell." He leaned back on his stool and gathered his thoughts. "We have gotten to the point where we've done about all we can do for you medically. The last option would be surgery to cut out the top rib on that right side. That may help relieve pressure on the nerves in your neck that are affecting that arm."

"So they just pop that top rib right out of there and that's supposed to fix everything?" I had never heard of such a thing. I think the thought threw me into shock.

"It is an option that you could pursue and it is my job to let you know what the options are. I didn't say it was a good option, but it is an option that you need to know about it."

After I thought about it for two seconds I said, "I don't think they will be sawing out my rib. That sounds awfully drastic in the hopes that it might do something."

"That answer works for me, and I think it's the right answer. When you have a flare up, call my office, and make an appointment."

"Well, if I am medically released, then it's time to start the settlement process, isn't it?"

"As long as it took you medically to get to this point," he paused "it will take twice as long to get through the legal process. With all that's going on, are you feeling depressed?" I shrugged. "Really, I am serious, because if you're not depressed, you're in denial."

"No. I don't know." I could feel the room getting smaller, my chest got tighter, tears started to fill my eyes. Part of me knew he was right, but the stubborn part of me had to be okay.

"If you aren't depressed, you are in denial." He repeated.

"I'm okay."

"When you need help, call me," he said.

We both knew I was still having problems, but as he said, that's about all medicine could do for me. He saw the signs, but I wasn't ready to accept that I might need an anti-depressant.

"The greater the power, more dangerous the abuse."
~ Edmund Burke (1729 – 1797)

Chapter 25

The Insurance Game Begins

When I was medically released, I called my friend, Tracy, the paralegal. Always my champion, she could help me breathe when I was freaking out.

"Are you really feeling okay? Really? Two years is pretty fast for all the injuries you had."

"Well, I'm told medicine has done all it can."

"Let me know when you're ready to proceed, and we can draw up a demand letter for you."

"So…what's a demand letter?"

"The demand letter is the first letter sent to the other driver's insurance company. It tells them we are representing you and demands settlement of the claim for a specific dollar amount. We need to collect your medical records so we can show cause for the demand amount."

"You have to remember this could be a long haul, Wendy. Since your injuries are soft-tissue, they're hard to prove. I need to warn you, this may not settle fast."

"I have already lost two and a half years of my life because of that damn wreck. I don't want to lose anymore. They know their client was at fault! When Dr. Benson treated me to the "best as medicine can get you" and medically released me, he said the legal process would take twice as long as the medical process."

There were days Tracy was the only reason I didn't jump off a bridge, and in the years to come, I would be in therapy for post-traumatic stress and anxiety disorders.

Worry, stress, and anxiety had become my middle names and I was depressed. Years of poking and prodding, tests and scans, doctors never agreeing, and constant pain and fatigue had taken their toll on me. Wasn't the worst part supposed to be over? Medicine had run out of answers. My regimen for maintenance consisted of physical therapy, chiropractic and tissue work, ice, heat, and painkillers, when I needed them.

As the legalities dragged on, I had many physical flare ups. The pain became so bad that I began receiving steroid injections when I needed them (not the same as spinal injections). The bursitis flare-ups were at the original injury sites; my shoulders, hips, and the SI joints, and my nervous system was shot.

I got to know how each of my symptoms worked, so I learned what I needed and when. Lying down all afternoon, every day, helped with fatigue, aches, and bowling-ball head. I learned that I had to maintain my physical improvements since the wreck. I could get my arms over my head and finally stretch without back spasms, most of the time. If I skipped three or four days of exercise, I would suffer. It felt like all the tissues inside shrunk up.

Amazing, this whole time I wanted to be better. After more than two years, I started to feel human again. I could sit up an hour or two at a time. I had done a lot of work in order to get myself better, and then, along came the insurance company wanting me to prove that I am broken. Part of me was stuck in that role while the rest of me was praying I could get my body back. I wanted to teach classes again. That would've been an interesting sight during a playshop or a class on movement, led by a teacher who couldn't move. Is that irony, or what?

Tracy called with the news that her firm had heard from the insurance company and they had requested my medical records. Looking at all my medical records was overwhelming. I closed my eyes and took a deep breath. "Thank you again, Lord. I am so glad I am not stuck somewhere in a coma. I have my limbs, although my brains are a bit scrambled. I could have died. I am so glad I didn't."

I knew I should write a book about all this. You get blindsided; no one has a clue what happens after the wreck; until it's way after. Surely I can help masses of people with a book that tells the story. Let them know they aren't alone. Educate people about techniques that may help them, like CranioSacral, Myofascial Release, and Atlas Orthogonal chiropractic. I don't understand why they aren't more mainstream.

Tracy was sure the medical records I had were more than enough for the insurance company.

"Okay, I've got the files. I'll get the letter finalized and you'll get your copy in the mail."

Time moved slowly as I waited for news about the insurance company. I continued the physical maintenance of my new body. When the bowling ball came around, it was time for some Atlas Orthogonal chiropractic. When they tapped that top vertebrae back under my skull, I could balance the bowling ball again. Seeing Lee for CranioSacral therapy afterward was great. She got the spinal fluid back in rhythm again with no more pressure than a nickel. Hold the right spots and the body will self-adjust. As I have said before, it's all connected.

It had been two years and eight months now. Perhaps the end was in sight and the light at the end of the tunnel was no longer an oncoming train.

Then it came; a very important-looking envelope. The demand letter the lawyer sent to the insurance company seemed pretty basic. Of course, in legal jargon, it sounded much more complicated. Basically it said, "Hi, I represent Wendy; your client buggered her up; medicine has done what it can; she's been released; and now it's time to pony up and pay the claim. Signed, Todd the lawyer."

As predicted, the insurance company responded within a week. At least they admitted she had insurance and they would be "investigating this loss accordingly." They wanted everything, the nature of the injury, treating doctors, medical bills, my medical status and current condition. They said to mail the medical bills and records so that they can "properly establish a settlement value." They were polite and even said please when requesting all the bills and medical records be forwarded to them. Everything was ready to go and was sent off within the week. The lawyer said to give them two months and see what happens.

After two months slipped by the lawyer sent a follow-up letter gently asking if they had the opportunity to review my medical records yet. The response took less than a week. The insurance company wrote to advise they were still processing and reviewing the medical bills and records. The letter stated, "We will contact you in the very near future."

The lawyer reminded me how slowly they moved and that this would take time. Four months passed, and there was still no response. The lawyer was starting to assume the insurance company would not settle.

When six months passed, the insurance company had still not made any contact, as they had indicated they would in their previous correspondence. I was in shock. I was outraged! How come they won't pay? Here are the doctors and here are the bills, it can't be that hard to add them up. We have to pay insurance premiums in order to drive legally, and then, when it comes time to cash in on the services we have been paying for all those years, you can't get a peep out of them, but that insurance premium bill still shows up every month. Why isn't that money spent paying settlements instead of lawyers? It's ridiculous they use our premiums to hire lawyers so they won't have to pay settlements. Pretty bizarre racket don't you think? And to think that man was so nice to me the day after the wreck. He told me not to worry, that she was insured and everything would be covered; my medical bills, my lost wages, they would pay to fix the car and we would look at pain-and-suffering. I believed him.

I knew time was short, and I would be handed off to another lawyer if the claim did not settle. The demand letters had been sent; the insurance company had all the information and ignored us for months. It was time to move forward and consider filing a lawsuit. The next week I received an email from Tracy telling me about the lawyer I was being referred to. She said he thought it was a good case, soft-tissue and all. Her email had all the information. His name was Artie Nelson. She included his phone number plus his paralegal's name. She said I would probably be talking with his paralegal, Sophie, more than I would him anyway.

Tracy told me to let them know I had been referred by Todd. She also told me that Artie was in trial and wouldn't be free for two or three weeks. She suggested I wait and call the next week to schedule an appointment.

The next week I made the call and scheduled an appointment a few weeks off with my new lawyer. I called Tracy to let her know. She suggested, "Why don't we have lunch that day? His office is only a couple blocks from ours."

"That works for me; it's a date."

"See you then; awesome!"

"See you then."

The lawyer's office was an hour from home. Fortunately, it was a beautiful drive which helped me ignore the pain in my right hip. I arrived at the firm where Tracy worked. We decided on burgers for lunch. Tracy could tell I was nervous. She kept reminding me that the new lawyer works for me. I felt calmer after lunch and the burgers were great. We finished lunch and headed back to her office. From her office she showed me where Artie's office was, about three blocks away. She gave me a "thumbs up" as thunder cracked from the sky.

"I think I'll drive."

"That sounds like a good idea. The sky looks pretty ominous."

I got into the car. I was lucky to find a parking place much closer to his office. I arrived and took a seat in the reception area. The woman across the room was sitting at a large desk talking on the phone. She nodded to let me know she knew I was there.

Two men were coming down the hall shaking hands. They had

a few parting comments and waved goodbye to each other.

"You must be Wendy Teague?"

"Yes, I am," I said sheepishly.

"Come on back to my office, and let's see what we've got." He had stacks of paperwork on his desk. He slapped his hand on a large pile and said, "This one is yours." He explained how things worked; how it would take time; and how I had to be patient. I told him Todd had already sent demand letters and I was referred to him because it was time for court. I read through the contract asking questions as we went, and then I signed it. It was pretty much how Tracy explained it. For sure, with this new lawyer, we were in business and this should be over soon. We would get a court date scheduled, right? Well…not exactly.

Three months later, that's four and a half years since my wreck, my new lawyer, Artie, sent his first demand letter to the insurance company. It was pretty much the same kind of letter that Todd had done the year before. "Hello, I'm representing Wendy. Now here's what's wrong and how screwed up she is, and this is the amount we want in order to settle."

That demand offer was good for forty-five days so it was back to "hurry up and wait." I never understood why he thought another demand letter would do any good. I had the understanding we were aiming straight for court. When I asked him why he had started with another demand letter, he said, "I would prefer to start off politely with the insurance company and hope they will settle without bringing in lawyers or going to court. They should have offered you at least $85,000 by now; we need a copy of her insurance policy so we can find out what the limits are. Getting a copy of that policy is key."

I asked what he meant by the limits.

"The limit of her insurance company's liabilities. If her insurance only covers $50,000 of damages, then that's all they are liable for."

"So they drag this out when they could just write a check?"

"You've got it."

Once again, the insurance company offered to settle my claim for $5,800. My lawyer was furious, and of course, so was I! He said he would contact them again to see if he could get that number higher. Some weeks later he told me they upped the offer to $6,200. He asked what I wanted to do.

"There is no reason for me to accept a settlement that won't cover my medical bills, they're over $30,000. That would be crazy. So what's the next step?"

"If you want to move ahead with the claim, it's time to file a petition for damages."

"Which is?"

"A petition for damages is filed with the court. When this gets filed, the insurance company is sure to call their lawyers. I will send you a copy of the petition along with five medical authorizations. Read through them, and let me know if we need to make any changes. When these are ready to go, you will have to sign all of them in front of a notary, and return them to my office."

I took a big gulp and agreed. The last year had been all "hurry up and wait." Perhaps this would light a fire under the insurance company so they will pay up.

"Do I return them certified?"

"Absolutely! Always!"

I received my copy of the petition for damages from the lawyer. When I started reading through it, I felt nauseated and angry that the insurance company wouldn't pay. Looks like we were headed to court; I was now a plaintiff and she was now a defendant. It was really rough emotionally to read the petition. It began with the when and how of the wreck. Then gut-wrenching phrases like, "and with great force, violently crashed into the right side of plaintiff's vehicle." My mind started swimming, and I found myself reliving the accident. I had to walk away before panic overtook me.

After a few hours, I gave it another try. The next section of the petition described the other driver's negligence and carelessness in four bullet points. The next section moved into listing my injuries; eleven bullet points stated that my neck was injured, my back was injured, my shoulders were injured and, when I read the next one, I felt paralyzed. It stated "The Plaintiff's entire nervous system, including the nerves and centers throughout her person, were injured, and thereby, caused to become damaged and diseased in all of the functions thereof impaired."

I couldn't catch my breath. I knew it was true but the legalese made me sound really broken. I could feel my denial fighting back; my mind still wouldn't admit my body was broken. It went on about how I had suffered, and will suffer, great physical pain and mental anguish in the future. The Plaintiff's general health, strength, and vitality have been injured and impaired. There were financial injuries, the medical expenses I incurred, and the money I lost because I had no income due to my injuries. It was only three and a half pages long, double spaced at that, and it took me a week to read it without crying.

I spoke with Sophie, Artie's paralegal, about a few changes and additions. After three weeks, the Petition for Damages was ready to file with the court. Artie mailed a copy and also included a list of the doctors and other providers as well as pharmacies where I received services. He informed me he would be requesting copies of all my records and billing statements and wanted me to check over the list to make sure he had it all correctly stated. I knew the list had to be complete, I recognized it the instant I saw it. It was the same one I had given to him in our first meeting and nothing had changed.

Now that the final Petition was ready, Jack drove me to the bank with the papers, which I signed, and the Public Notary affixed his seal to it and politely thanked me. I folded the papers and sealed them in the ready-envelope as Jack drove to the post office. I walked into the post office, handed my letter to the mailman and said "Certified mail please."

"You've got it," he said from behind the counter.

I was exhausted and, when we got home, I had a good cry on Jack's shoulder and then slept for hours. I don't thank Jack enough for everything he does. Thank you, Jack, you are my hero!

Two weeks later I received notice from Artie. We were scheduled with the court for a Case Management Conference in three months. In layman's terms, that's legal for a meeting. All that was left to do was to serve notice to the woman and her insurance company about the conference. It was exciting to think that after seven months with Artie, the insurance company would finally pay the bills, like they said they would, after having dragged their feet for years.

We hit our first snag when the insurance company wouldn't recognize Artie as my lawyer when he sent out his demand letter. That meant more paperwork for us, and more billable hours for them. Todd submitted a letter stating he was no longer representing me, and Artie submitted a letter stating he was my new lawyer. Small snag; surely things will go smoothly now.

Three months later, we had another scheduled conference. We had not been able to locate the woman who hit me. The judge asked if we knew her location and my lawyer responded, "We believe she has moved to Aruba." All the lawyers started laughing and offered to go take the deposition. I wanted to smack them all!

The case management conference was postponed for another three months. I wasn't happy. I asked the lawyer, "Why does it matter? The insurance company told me they would pay medical bills, lost wages, fix the car, plus pain and suffering. Why do we need to serve her with a summons, her insurance knows she had a wreck and it was her fault. So why don't they just pay? That's why we pay car insurance, isn't it?"

"In a perfect world," he said with a smirk on his face. "We have to serve her with a summons to go forward. She is actually the one liable for the claim that her insurance company insured her for. We need her to contact us, or them, so we can move forward. Their offer still stands at $6,200, which is ridiculous. We need to find her."

I was stymied. "Her insurance company doesn't know where she is, so that makes it our problem? Why is that our problem? She's their client, she pays premiums to them."

"They have no motivation to find her. When she contacts them, they'll have to get in the ballgame."

"Okay." I felt helpless. I kept remembering Dr. Benson saying, "The legal process will take twice as long as the medical took." I was beginning to understand. I was so excited to get this conference done. The joke was on me.

After the case management meeting, I headed downstairs to call Jack. There were no phones. I asked a woman behind the desk for a phone and she said, "I'm sorry, there are no pay phones. The phone company took them out some time ago."

"No phones? There are no phone booths in the whole courthouse," I was stunned! I miss clean safe phone booths.

A kind gentleman heard my plea and said, "Do you need a phone?"

"I just need to call my ride."

"Here, use mine."

"Oh, thank you so much! I had no idea they had no payphones here."

He smiled.

The next year was like a broken record. Oh we have another court date! What? Still haven't found her? Postponed again? I was told of a bizarre law: if she doesn't contact her insurance company and they cannot find her, she can be classified as a "non-cooperative client," and when they have a case with a non-cooperative client and the client never contacts them, they may not be liable for anything. Now that's ridiculous! I think that was more of our premium money working against us. It got to the point where I was afraid to go outside. I was paranoid that the insurance company was always watching me. When I told my lawyer that, he said, "It's possible."

Finally, court came again. "What? $20,000? That doesn't cover my bills, why should I settle for that? That's ridiculous. I have doctor bills and my health insurance company wants their money back, so why should I settle for $20,000? That would be stupid."

"I was trying to get you some cash. I know how tight things are for you."

"I don't just want some cash, I want what it should be, not pennies on the dollar. I will never be the same again, ever! My body will never be the same again! So why are they treating me so badly when their client smashed into my car and spun me like a top?" I was furious! I could feel all my muscles starting to seize up.

"She has another case file; I'll see if I can track down the investigator who found her for that one."

"I don't understand this."

Another three months went by, and I was at court again at eight in the morning. I'm not a morning girl, especially after coming to all my court dates and wasting my time. This time I took a seat in the third row. There were two lawyers standing in the front row in their $1,200 suits and I heard one of them say, "Oh these people - they always think the insurance company is the bad guy," she said smiling. She didn't talk quietly either; I heard every word she said. Being on the other side it felt like she was making fun of people.

When they glanced around, I glared at them and said, "Some of us have a reason to feel that way. You should be careful who you say that around." I know my expression made an impression. They quickly moved to the other side of the room.

There were approximately eleven times court was rescheduled with Artie over the course of a year and a half. I was worn to a frazzle. I think the insurance company's goal was to make me settle for pennies, or just go away. Artie spoke with me about another lawyer, a friend from college whose law firm only took personal injury cases like mine. I was so frustrated, I was happy to change lawyers. I think he was happy to get rid of my case. Bring on the new guy.

We had our next hearing three months later. Artie said that his friend, Kit Cameron, would be there that day so I could meet him. He agreed to take on my case for trial.

Once again, the hearing was a waste of time. Unfortunately, it was one of those days where everything hurt, and I was in the bad mood. When I heard the judge announce another postponement, I started to cry. I was so frustrated and angry and disappointed and overwhelmed. What a great day to meet my new lawyer.

After court, when we were standing in the hall, I looked up at Artie and said, "Do you realize your firm and I have been through two weddings, three babies, and a broken hip together?" He cocked his head thinking and said, "Wow that sounds about right." I think he saw a new way of looking at time through a client's eyes.

He waved, "There's Kit; come on down here." Artie introduced me to my new lawyer, Kit Cameron, personal injury lawyer number three. Artie excused himself for his next case, and Kit and I sat down on the bench.

By this point I was crying and was a mess. He waited patiently for me to calm down and then started asking questions. We sat there talking in the hallway. He already had my file and asked me a few questions to make sure he had what he needed to get started. He even had me read and sign the contingency fee contract right there. Artie filed papers withdrawing himself as my lawyer, and Kit filed papers that he was my new lawyer.

It's amazing how expensive having a car wreck is, even when it's not my fault. The insurance company will not pay a penny until it's time for a settlement, and it's not time for a settlement until you know what's wrong with you and what your future health concerns will most likely be. Don't settle too fast! Some injuries can take months to surface.

"Real knowledge is to know the extent of one's ignorance."
~ Confucius (551 BC – 479 BC)

Chapter 26

Do You Know What's in Your Medical Records?

Have you ever actually seen your medical records? Do you know what's in them?

I was medically released, with restrictions, two and a half years after my accident. The I.M.E. report took months, and then Dr. Benson treated me for three more months. I once asked why the report took so long and he replied, "I don't have the power to subpoena. Lawyers can subpoena records, but I have to rely on doctors to send them. I have no way to make them send me your records. Some offices move very slowly." He even requested that I call a couple of them to see if I could get them to send my records to him.

When Dr. Benson medically released me, I remember he said, "You're as well as medicine can get you, period. Call me when you need me and good luck on the legal side. Just so you know it usually takes twice as long as the medical."

"Oh great, something new to "hurry up and wait" for," I had said sarcastically.

"It will take as long as it takes," he said. "Good luck." Dr. Benson was actually quite nice after the final report was completed. He had changed from the serious examiner to my doctor.

Now it was time for me to gather records for the lawyer. I kept a list of all the doctors and hospitals I had been to, so that's where I started. I called ahead to see if they had my records, how long it would take to get a copy, and what the cost would be. Most of my files were so small, there was no charge. One set cost $35 plus an hour of my drive time. I never thought to ask Dr. Benson for a copy of my file; it would have contained everything.

My file at Dr. Sebastian's office was huge. She laughed when I handed her a ream of copy paper.

"You didn't have to do that."

"I feel bad. My file is probably two reams of paper."

"Don't worry, there are guidelines for that; we can charge for records" she said. You're file is so large, it will take several weeks to get everything copied."

"Okay, I will let Dr. Benson's office know."

I had to sign a release for every set of my own records. All the different piles became overwhelming. I read the records as I gathered them. It's amazing what doctors put in your files that you have no clue about. I had a checkup nine months after the wreck. As usual, the doctor was too busy, so I scheduled with a nurse practitioner. I wanted to talk about my issues from the accident, and it was time for a wellness checkup. I was still having headaches and severe neck and back problems and pain. Reading and math were still a problem. A serious side effect of the pain medication was constipation. When I scheduled my appointment, I told them that I was having pain and diverticulitis symptoms that needed attention, as well.

When I reported for my wellness appointment, I reminded them of the other problems I was having. They didn't seem to have time for anything but the wellness protocol. She did put some of my remarks in my records and started me on an antibiotic for the diverticulitis but gave me nothing for pain. She asked, "How's your sex life?"

"I haven't had sex since the wreck. It still hurts to get a hug." It made me feel sad.

When I read her records, my jaw dropped. She had noted my sex life as "normal." Did she just not listen? It's a wellness appointment, so we follow the template and nothing else counts? Sometimes I forget there is no diagnosis code for "spoke with my patient for ten minutes" or "my patient is healthy." If there's no diagnosis code, the doctor can't bill the insurance company.

I scheduled another appointment with my MD six months later. I had myself all worked up, a definite sign I needed a new doctor, but this was the one I had for now. I couldn't see changing doctors during the settlement process. It wouldn't be fair to the new doctor. I was still having pain, headaches when I read, and I was still learning how to write again. I was convinced it was Shaken Baby Syndrome on the adult level. The car shook me like a blender; forward, backwards, sideways, and in circles.

When I brought up having a concussion with the doctor, she asked, once again, if I had hit my head. Once again I answered, "I don't know."

"If you didn't hit your head, you wouldn't have had a concussion."

She noted in the file that she didn't think my brain issues had anything to do with the wreck. I was stunned! She never gave me any clue as to what she thought was going on. She just handed me off to another doctor when I complained about problems from the wreck. Also in the file was the neurologist's letter suggesting it may be a fascia issue, but I was never told that.

I read through test results that indicated I was "left-hand dominant" and then said I was "right-hand dominant." Another doctor noted that I was taking a specific over-the-counter pain reliever that I can't take because it gives me dreadful headaches. I had no idea that my medical records were so screwed up. In fact, I had a close friend who was shocked when he was turned down for life insurance because he has asthma. I've known this man for decades, and he has never had asthma. Why was that in his medical records? Do doctors just pick a diagnosis code for billing?

I knew the medical records I collected would not count as official documents, but I was able to read them to find out what was in them. When the settlement process finally started, I had to pay for certified copies from the doctor. That goes under legal expenses. I suppose that's so they were sure I didn't change them. Chain of evidence, I guess, plus it's billable hours for the other side, if they request their own copies. What a waste of resources!

Once upon a time I found out I had been diagnosed with fibro cystic breast disease. I left my doctor's office and walked to the checkout desk. When I looked down and saw that diagnosis on my sheet, I turned around and marched right back to the doctor and asked him, "What's this?"

"Oh that's no big deal; most women your age have that."

"Why didn't you tell me that when I was in here?"

"It's nothing for you to worry about. I have another patient now," he said rudely. I had been dismissed. So that diagnosis was in my records, and I don't know if I actually have it or not. I think I was "labeled" simply to bill the insurance company.

Once it's in your medical records how do you get it out? It's pretty tough to do when you don't even know it's in there. I have to admit…having everyone's medical records in the electronic "Never Never Land" scares the hell out of me. I operated computers for twenty years and I know that a computer will only do what you tell it to do. One comma or one period out of place and a computer can make as many mistakes in twenty seconds as it takes twenty men twenty years to make. It's only a matter of time until the insurance companies find a way to get their mitts on our electronic health information; just another file to be hacked.

Frightening, don't you think?

I could list more problems with medical records, but I think you get my point.

Do you know what's in your medical records? Just saying…

"There is no greater sorrow than to recall
happiness in times of misery."
~ Dante Alighieri (1265 – 1321)

Chapter 27

Facing Chronic Issues Head On

When I look back at my notes, seven years after the wreck, it amazes me I still feel like crap, so much of the time. It's as if I can't find my inner strength, my energy, or my power. I looked at the journal I kept until my medical release. Many times I wondered why I didn't keep it going, and then I remember how tired I became of writing about all the pains of the days. It only reinforced that I am broken and this is the best I will ever be. Every day, when I wrote down all my episodes of pain and spasms, they were being reinforced by my writing about them. I was medically released. I didn't know I needed to keep taking notes. Had I known then how long everything would take, I would have kept up with the notes but, then again, my notes were used against me. If you keep notes, let the doctor see them but DO NOT allow them to be placed in your medical file!

I started my notes in March of 2004 and backtracked to the crash date in February. The last page was dated Monday, June 26, 2006. I made a note: Ortho on June 26 and chiropractor on June 27. The last page was a basic listing of what I could and couldn't do when I was medically released.

The first column read:

After last visit, hurt rest of day
Get really excited - neck tightens up even more
Neck rolls make discs worse?
Neck really tired!
Math still not good
Problem solving/mechanical/cognitive brain still not good
Do well with consistent breaks and a mid-day horizontal break
Still get that "snapped in half" crunchy feeling in mid-back
when very tired

The next column began with all CAN DO:

Weed slowly and carefully, take breaks
Fill no more than one plastic grocery bag
Get hose out and reel up - some days exhausting! Some days
I'm down for days! (The hose usually wins)
Can finally wear very light, small pendants
Pilates Performer machine — half routine
Chi Gong moves
Sit up in bed, but only for five minutes

And the third column began with CANNOT DO:

Go Full Speed
Curl up
Lie down and prop head on hand/elbow
Thong sandals — make my hips hurt
Let hair get long — too heavy — too much pressure on my neck
Yard work for more than fifteen minutes
Look up or down very long, like looking at the sky or reading
Heavy jewelry — anything around my neck
Jump or hop around
Spin around in the kitchen to different cabinets (small kitchen)
Hang cordless phone on T-shirt (too heavy on neck)

Interestingly, the journal entry for Monday, June 26, 2006 was about going to the Ortho. The doctor said to learn my limitations, take breaks through the day, and stick with what works. He could tell how much pain I was in when we first met and now he can tell I am doing much better. He also said to keep up with chiropractic when I need it and stick to what I was doing.

The last entry was Tuesday, June 27, 2006 - Woke with a killer headache, took shower, Dr. Gallo at 11:30.

It was April of 2010. I was stunned these notes were from four years ago. When I was preparing to write this chapter on a class I took about dealing with chronic problems, it seemed as though it had only been a couple years since the wreck, but here it was seven years later. It's bizarre to see how fast time has gone.

The rest of the world hadn't stopped for me. I felt as though life was slipping through my fingers and there was nothing I could do to fix any of it. I felt left behind by life. Regardless of all the doctors who assured me I would never be the same, I still wondered if my body could ever be the same as it was before the wreck.

Natasha, Nat for short, has been a friend for years, way before the wreck. She performs hypnosis, past-life regression, and emotional release techniques.

Nat was teaching a course on dealing with chronic issues. "This class would be great for you! We are doing it in three locations, so you can choose where you'd like to take the class. I think one is pretty close to your Mom's. That would help you out. You wouldn't have to drive so far in one day if you stayed with her."

I was interested in the class and more than happy to support her in her new venture. All the work Nat has done with me over the years has been amazing. I knew I would learn something.

Nat continued with excitement, "It's only one day a week for six weeks. All you have to cover is the book." Her passion was infectious.

"Nat, I'll have to miss one of the classes."

"One of the requirements is to attend every session," Nat responded.

"I have to do a deposition the third week. This insurance legal game has gone on so long, I can't not go, and I can't change the appointment."

"I will talk to the other teacher and see if she is okay with it. I don't see a problem and you're right - you don't want to reschedule that, not after all this time. How long has it been? At least two or three years, right?"

I counted on my fingers. "Let's see, 04, 5, 6, 7, 8, 9, 10, that makes seven years. Can you believe that?"

"That's ridiculous; you should have had that settlement ages ago."

"Yeah, tell me about it. Insurance companies! I finally stopped holding my breath. I am trying to move forward and get some kind of life going. Sounds like a good class. Send me the e-mail, I'll check it out."

"We're still working on the flyer. It's a great class; all about self-managing chronic issues. You know, like the ones you've had since the wreck."

Knowing I was still denying all the ways my life had changed, I could hear the passion in her voice, along with a little sarcasm.

She knew what I had gone through. She felt this was another way to help heal me.

She kept on encouraging me to take the class. "The only cost would be for the book. It's self-help Wendy. It's about self-management. The course will give you more understanding of the effects of chronic problems and has techniques that help you deal with how life is now; things you can do to make your life easier while learning how to do things differently. I really think you will get a lot out of it!" She continued with more details. When the flyer arrived in my inbox, I signed up.

I was anxious; wondering if I could handle a class every week. From home it was a thirty-minute drive; from Mom's, only fifteen minutes. The first week I drove to Mom's, then to the meeting, and back to Moms; all in the same day and it was way too much for me. All the driving and sitting made me ache for days. So I started driving to Mom's the day before class and home the day after. It gave me time to rest and recoup between drives with ice packs and painkillers.

The first week we went over the basics. Acute means there is a beginning and an end. Chronic goes on and on. I was chronic with acute episodes. Whichever issues I was dealing with, it was my job to learn how to self-manage my life so it worked for me. Let go of what I can't do and embrace what I can do. And remember to take breaks when I need them! It's okay to ask for help. We were encouraged to honor ourselves by getting up whenever we needed to. I did my best to stand and stretch every half hour.

I was reminded it is MY JOB to take care of my own health, whether it's getting my medications adjusted or going for a second opinion. No one knows my body better than I do. My health is my responsibility. It was time to let the denial go. It was also time to manage my activities. Okay, so "I can't" will be replaced with "I can" and "I will!"

Emotions that stem from chronic issues were discussed, as were frustrations that came from learning that my new body can't do all the things it did before. Each of us, regardless of the issue, has emotions. Physical pain is one thing, but when those emotions kicked in too, it started playing a whole new game in my head that led to depression. I resisted the thought that my problems were chronic. I thought if I believed I was chronic, I would never get better.

Chronic illnesses don't always have predictable patterns. You learn what to avoid, but some days the pain comes and goes at will. It can be quite overwhelming. Cooking a simple meal can be exhausting. I don't remember the joy of standing up, arms over my head, stretching as far as I could with no back spasms. I am so glad Jack loves me and that he's a good cook too!

My injuries are what they are and it's time to deal with it! My body tenses up in different areas and different ways. My neck constricts and shrinks in pain. My muscles tense up in painful spasms.

The pain indulges the anxiety that "this will never be over." I stress out over paying bills with credit cards. I feel helpless. The difficult emotions like anger and frustration are all in there too. Self-doubt and self-criticism slip in, and then it's hard to trust anything. Feeling helpless and not being able to trust my own body also leads to depression.

I love to lie tucked under the covers hiding from the world; trying to hide from this new reality that has become my life. Sometimes I would hide for weeks. I was exhausted from all the negative emotions and the pain. Once my body relaxed again, it was only a matter of time until something triggered another spasm. I had no control over it. Some nights my calves tightened up so badly that my feet curled out. Walking was excruciating, but I would force myself to stand up and walk until my feet went flat again.

I was apprehensive about the class, but I showed up. Everything shared was valuable. It was amazing to see these ladies teaching the class and being such inspirational role models. They understood what we were talking about; they had issues too. Over the weeks they shared so many tools about physical activity, planning better, managing pain, healthy eating, and the right doctors.

Understanding our emotions, good or bad, without judgment, is a huge challenge. Feeling my feelings was a crucial part of understanding I had to admit my life had changed dramatically. I had to figure out who I am now. I had to figure out what was a sustainable level for me physically. Understanding my own chronic cycle empowers me as I move forward with my life.

It's okay to open the flood gates and let everything come pouring out. Keeping it all inside will not help you or the ones around you. Trauma changes you, like the pebble under the water. Years without a great hug from Jack...how do you mend that? Those moments are gone forever. No amount of money from the Insurance Company can replace them.

Every year I continue to get a little better. Jack doesn't squeeze me or hug me, still afraid of hurting me. He is still hanging in there with me after all these years and he still loves me. How do you bring the intimacy back when both of us are afraid of pain?

After just one class, I knew it would help me start being gentle with myself and help me learn to self-manage my issues. Early on, we were taught the simple art of distraction to get through short activities. Distraction works because it's hard on your brain to do two things at once, like patting your head and rubbing your stomach. Simple distractions include taking a few minutes to breathe, positive self-talk in the mirror, prayer, or meditation. Distraction can be a simple tool for caretakers as well.

I assist the making of new neurotransmitters in my brain and reinforcing them with positive thought as much as I can. When I walk down the stairs in the morning I talk to myself, "Okay hip, we can make it down these stairs. It's easy." I send myself healing energy by repeating the thought "I can do it." It's not easy to be in the good mood everyone is used to when you're in pain and exhausted all the time.

One of the best distractions is laughing. Laughing releases endorphins in your brain that help you feel better. You can start off with a fake laugh; your brain can't tell the difference. I used to laugh a lot. I miss that Wendy. I felt this class was going to change my life as much as the wreck did. I was fortunate to be a part of it.

Before we parted, we discussed action plans and goal setting — what to do next week to improve our own lives. If the goal was a large project, it might be easier and save overwhelm by breaking the large project into smaller, more reasonable goals. For example, adding a treadmill to your exercise routine is great. However, you would not walk a mile the very first time. Start at however long you can do it comfortably. Set the goal to walk ten minutes a day, every other day; or commit to walking three minutes a day. Perhaps walk to your mailbox every day.

I was staring at that piece of paper pondering what my goals would be. They needed to be obtainable. Setting one goal a week that I felt comfortable with seemed impossible. Later my goal would be to break down a large project into chunks.

The goals include the what, how much, when, and how often. Don't set the goals too high. Make them reasonable. Be gentle with yourself. If the goal was to walk ten minutes and you actually walked fifteen minutes, the extra five minutes is gravy! Knowing you can only do five minutes and setting your goal for ten minutes only sets you up for failure. We needed goals we could accomplish. It is amazing how good it feels to actually accomplish something, to feel I had accomplished something.

I love playing in the dirt and working with plants. Dr. Gallo restricted me to a container garden, and only one container a day. I have had a nice container garden for about six years now. I can only play every two or three days, and for a very short time. This week my action plan was to inventory my plants and pots, and to enjoy being outside for three days for thirty minutes. My goals were set for the week.

All that information in one day was an awful lot to take in. Thankfully I had the book to use and reference at home and the teachers were available if we needed help during the week. I learned to set guidelines, be gentle with myself, and it was amazing. I actually believed I could achieve something. For so long I was in pain, not really living life.

Problem-solving was next. Of course, you first have to identify what the problem is before you can solve it, and to identify the problem, you have to be willing to admit that there is a problem. For years I put up with all this pain and was still resistant to admitting I had a problem. Once you can admit it, start brainstorming, both in and out of the box. No limits! Don't judge anything, everything is possible. Write down all the ideas you come up with and look at what you have now and what you are capable of doing, right now. Figure out what came up in your brainstorming session that meets your needs. What can you do to solve your own problems?

Before we took a break, I asked, "Does anyone else feel like there's a buzz saw in their head? I will be on the edge of sleep, and then a sound like a buzz saw zips through my brain and jars me awake. It's a strange feeling that's gone as fast as it came. It's a startling experience." I saw three heads bobbing in agreement. Although we really didn't discuss what it was, I felt better knowing I was not alone.

Accountability came next. Without accountability, humans tend to take the easy way out and live a life of procrastination. It's my job to learn self-management; no one can do that for me. I must be willing to be accountable for my actions. When you give your word, do your best to show up. If it's one of those days when everything hurts, give yourself permission to cancel the day and cuddle with your ice packs. I think the toughest things to regain, after feeling like I didn't matter for years, were self-love and self-respect. I still didn't feel whole. I still didn't really have a life. Seven years, that's a long time to be in pain. It changes you.
There are so many emotions involved. Until you've been there you don't really understand. The frustration of losing physical abilities and mental faculties made me angry.

For some time, I worried more about the driver who hit me than about myself; always hoping she would be fine. One day Mom said, "Stop worrying about her; this wasn't your fault. She ran into you, remember? This wasn't your fault."

Amazing isn't it…that I would be more worried about her? She was nice, and she did ask how I was, but after that day at the police station, I never saw her again. Then, during all the legal stuff, I was informed she had moved out of the country. Yes I had a lot of emotions brewing! I wasn't as depressed anymore, that was nice. However, the anxiety attacks came up more often and were getting worse. This was a good group for me to be in.

After discussing emotions and our own negative self-talk, we moved into a more positive subject…tools to lift you up on down days. Have a discussion with myself in the mirror. Make the commitment that I will never give up. Pay attention to myself and honor myself. If there is a problem, don't procrastinate, deal with it. Stay as active as you can. Physical activity is good, as long as your doctor approves. We went through a few physical movements to help with balance and coordination and it was suggested that one hundred and twenty minutes of stretching and moving a week is a good goal to start with. That's only two hours during the entire week. Stretching and movement can sometimes even stop some pain. It's a good way to improve flexibility, strength, and endurance; and exercising at your own level and speed may help improve your mood too. The achievement feels great. Some days I even felt human again.

Slowly, bit by bit, you can see the small goals that will help complete your larger vision. Set a goal and work up to it every week. Exercise is also good for keeping your bodily fluids moving and to help with mobility. There is no magic bullet out there, so find what works for you. Body movement is vital! Enjoy what you are doing; visualize your muscles toning themselves.

I used to teach classes in sound and movement. I knew how my body could move before the wreck. Unfortunately, none of my medical team knew me then. Some things are still very difficult, like lifting a two liter bottle of soda. A gallon of milk was off-limits. Nothing bigger than two quarts; some days are still very difficult. When the cartilage between that right rib head and the breastbone is inflamed, I am useless and usually in agony.

I came up with some powerful statements for positive reinforcement during class:

I empower myself with exercise.

Each movement improves my health. I feel better.
I manage my life better with exercise. Exercise works, I keep it
up.
I regenerate and rejuvenate with my breathing movement.
I increase my flexibility, strength, and endurance.
Exercise makes me feel better every day.
I am full of positive energy!

I was talking with a gal I had connected with during class. She
said, "If this is you with brain damage, you must have been
really smart before!"

I grinned "I was a computer programmer analyst for 20 years."

"Wow — now that takes some brains. Can you still do that kind
of work?"

"No, not really. My mechanical and analytical brains seem to
have been disconnected in the wreck. It's like all the connections
are off just a hair. It took me months to learn how to write again.
I can read, but not very well, and my math is still awful."

"I want to give you a card for another class. This one is for grief.
It feels like you have a lot to let go of that you haven't really
faced yet. I teach a class here and another one at your end of
town."

"That would certainly be closer, but I don't understand why I
would need a grief class."

"I don't feel like you have allowed yourself to grieve any of
what's going on. Think about it. You have really been through a
lot for a long time and you're acting like a Pollyanna. You need
to face it head on."

I took the card from her, "I will think about it." I looked down at the card, "This starts in two weeks, wow, that's fast" I said and filed the card in my notebook. She's probably right, I thought, as I started the car and headed off to Mom's.

This is only my second week and I am exhausted from all the travel and all the input. Granted, at most it's only a thirty-minute drive, but it's a real long thirty minutes for me, and then to drive home again? That's a long trip when cars freak you out...true story!

The grief class started the week after my deposition. Maybe it would be a good idea. It didn't cost anything and it was only about ten minutes from home. I found the card in my notebook and slowly began staring at the names and the locations. It was a ten-week format starting the fourth week of this chronic class. That meant two weeks with two classes. I could attend the grief class on Tuesdays, drive to Mom's later in the afternoon, and rest before the chronic class the next day. I dialed the phone and signed up. When I hung up, I wondered if I could really pull off two classes at the same time, with a deposition thrown in there to boot, but that's another chapter, literally.

The third week I surprised Nat when I walked into class. She watched me set my books on the table. I could feel her eyes on me. I turned and said, "The deposition was canceled, so I thought I'd come." Nat came over to me and said, "I am sorry it was cancelled. Have they set up another one yet?"

"No, it's all "hurry up and wait" again. The lawyer will let me know when it's rescheduled. The gal moved out of the country and they still haven't found her. Ain't that a bitch?" I was fuming!

Nat said, "Look at me, c'mon Wendy, look at me." I turned my gaze in her direction and we locked eyes. "Now" she paused, "take a nice deep breath." I did. "Now take another one...and another one…" Her gaze never wandered from my eyes as she took each breath with me. "How do you feel now?"

"Still angry, but more grounded."

"Good," she said.

"Thank you." The room was starting to fill up. I took my seat. People smiled when they saw me. "We thought you weren't coming today?"

"The deposition was cancelled again so here I am."

"So glad you got to come today."

Today we would be discussing different aspects of soft-tissue pain, the importance of breathing, and learning to schedule your life. Deep breathing uses your diaphragm, gets things pumping, and increases oxygen in the body. Interesting how breath-work made my flashbacks of the wreck more frequent.

Whatever physical activity you prefer, include walking. When starting out you may be able to walk for five minutes without feeling a lot of fatigue. After five minutes of activity, rest. Hopefully, after thirty minutes of rest, you will feel completely recovered from the workout. If not then start smaller, with just a couple of minutes and work your way up to five minutes.

Being fit has to do with consistency. How many times a week do you exercise, how hard do you work, and how much exercise do you get each day. Warm up before any work out and don't work too hard. Do what you can do comfortably. I feel activity should definitely be a part of pain and fatigue management on whatever level you are. Breathing feeds the body, the lungs pump the oxygen into the body, and the body moves. We truly are amazingly created.

There are things you can do for yourself and you don't have to pay anybody to help you do them. Simple things like cutting back on caffeine, letting go of stress, exercising, deep breathing, laughter, and music are all wonderful self-management techniques your doctor may never suggest.

This week we were to track our daily physical activity. I could only handle activity for a maximum of thirty minutes and then I would need a horizontal break for at least an hour to rest my neck and back. Fascinating, when I wrote everything down, I could see I was doing more than I thought living thirty minutes at a time.

Communication skills were also discussed. By identifying what really bothers me and expressing my feelings, my needs have a better chance of being met because others will know what I need when I share it with them. It is okay to ask for help.

There are four reasons for medications. The most common medications are used to relieve symptoms. Some medicines may help prevent further problems. Some actually improve or slow down a disease process, while others replace what your body no longer makes. If you are able, take responsibility for your medications. When discussing your situation with your doctor or health care provider, make sure they are aware of all your medications, the dosage, and if you take anything over-the-counter. Discuss the need for each medication and if they are still appropriate or perhaps no longer needed. It is also a good idea to use the same pharmacy, so they have all your medications on file and may catch medications that don't mix.

My Mom gave me a great tip. She carries a small card in her wallet that lists her medication and their dosages. So I typed up my medications on a small card and laminated it to keep in my wallet. Jack has a copy too. It's much easier to remember medications and dosages if you have them written down and already prepared. If any of your medications are giving you problems, report the effects to your health care provider as soon as possible. You need to stay in charge, it's your body and you know how it works, how it feels, and how your different medications affect you.

Another big issue discussed was the depression that occurs with chronic issues. Symptoms can manifest differently in different people. Some turn to food while others turn away from food. Food is one of the few things they feel they have any control over. Depression may show itself as mood swings, feelings of hopelessness, and constant arguments. There were days of dark thoughts, of wanting to hit someone, wanting to hit anything, wanting to know why the woman who hit me left the country before this was done. I couldn't believe she left the country. She knew she creamed me. I don't understand why she wouldn't keep in touch to make sure it was taken care of. She paid her insurance premiums, so why haven't they paid me. Then there's the rare dark day filled with dark thoughts thinking through the pros and cons of suicide. No, I never admitted that to doctors. I didn't want to be locked up and I knew I would never actually do it.

I understand it is important to deal with depression. It's such a heavy subject; it makes the whole room heavy. Fortunately, after the break, we moved into positive thinking. We fed ourselves positive energy like "I am an able person," "I feel better about myself every day," "Having challenges doesn't mean I can't do things," and "It may not be easy—but I can do it!" Learn to break down projects into bite-sized pieces you and your body can handle without harming yourself. It will help you utilize your energy better, another purpose for goal setting every week. How do you utilize the energy you still have and how effectively do you use it? Be honest with yourself in your goal setting; be realistic with yourself. It was awful for me to be honest and speak out loud about how screwed up my life was because of my car wreck. It's still hard to accept.

The next two weeks were exhausting. I would attend the grief class then drive to Mom's before rush hour started. The next day I had my chronic issue class and stayed at Mom's another night before coming home. My energy felt depleted. I love staying at Mom's. I am happy to say we are great buds! I was exhausted from my schedule of driving and thinking so much every week. The chronic class was over. I had another eight weeks of grief class much closer to home. It was nice to lie around and rest in my own house and my own bed. Instead of being gone for days every week, I was only gone for a couple of hours. It was a welcome change!

"Diseases of the soul are more dangerous than those of the body."

~ Cicero (106 BC – 43 BC)

Chapter 28

Coming Face to Face with Grief

It was the first day of my grief class. I surfed the web for the location and it was only about fifteen minutes from home. I hadn't been there before, didn't know what I would be walking into, and I was getting anxious. On top of that, I had to drive to Mom's for the chronic class tomorrow. It was overwhelming. The car was packed and I was ready to head over to Mom's after class. I almost chickened out, but I made myself go.

When I arrived, people were very friendly and pointed me in the right direction for the group. I walked down the hall and ducked into the bathroom. I looked at myself in the mirror and said, "You can do this, don't be a wuss." I splashed water on my face and ran my fingers through my hair. When I felt calmer, I headed slowly to the classroom.

I signed in, met the facilitator, and received the book for group. When my turn came to introduce myself, I felt very out of place.

"I'm not sure I should be here. I am the only one here who has not lost a loved one. I am here because a friend thought this would be a good place for me to deal with my grief after a car wreck."

The facilitator spoke up, "Wendy, how long ago was the wreck?"

"A little over seven years."

"And tell us how that wreck changed your life?"

"Nothing is the same. My strength and stamina are gone. I can't think and figure out problems anymore. My brain still just doesn't work right." At that point my eyes were flooded with tears. Tissue boxes came from both sides. I think I was finally starting to accept my life would never be the same.

"Okay, Wendy, you're life has been forever changed. That is certainly something to grieve. In this room we do not compare our grief to anyone else's. Every person deals with grief in their own way. Wendy, welcome to our group. I hope you continue to come and join us each week."

We split into small groups to tell our stories. When I moved to my group, a young lady reached across the table and gently put her hand on my forearm. Quietly she said, "Don't you ever doubt that you belong in this group. You had a car wreck, you lost your life! Everything is different! You have every right to be here to grieve for the life that you lost and don't you ever let anyone else tell you otherwise."

This person, who I had never met before, touched me so deeply. She was an angel. It struck me…I'd been in the chronic class for weeks and all it took was the simple words of that young lady to bring me to tears. In the chronic group, we addressed emotions, but not in the way this grief class did in the first fifteen minutes.

When our meeting was over, we came back together joining hands in a circle, and in closing our group for the day, the facilitator gave us a few guidelines to work with.

"One, be honest with yourself! If you're not willing to be honest, you will not be able to clear out the grief. Number two, don't compare yourself with anyone else; every person is unique. Grief is a normal, natural reaction to loss, and remember, your loss is important and so is your grief. The loss and grief are both yours. There are no absolutes. There is no wrong way to grieve. However, when you move through grief, you move into a healthier life." With that, we said our goodbyes until next week.

Again I stopped in the bathroom and ran cool water over my face. Silly I know, but I didn't want Jack to see me with my eyes red from crying. I sat in the car for a few minutes. My world had been rocked. I knew it would be a long day, but I had no idea it would go so deep.

I came home to a tender, loving hug from Jack. We chatted for a bit and then he loaded the car for me. A kiss and off I headed to Mom's before it got any later; the less traffic the better. Some days the anxiety was so high, I couldn't get near the car. This would be my fourth trip to Mom's house in as many weeks. I was feeling quite pooped. Ironically, this was the week that the chronic class would be addressing depression management. All the driving was catching up with me. I stayed an extra night that week to celebrate Mother's Day early.

Mom and I have a great relationship. We're always glad to see each other. I also knew each time I drove out that I would have to drive back home. I think all that driving kept me in overload. I was always afraid of other drivers; never knowing if someone would run into me again.

The homework from the grief class was much harder than any I had in the chronic class. The chronic class was helping me deal with the fact that my body was so different since the wreck and it couldn't do what it used to. The grief classes helped me face the truth and look at the mental and emotional effects of the wreck. I wasn't the same person. I lost my colors. My life lost its color. For years my favorite shirt was a long, bright, tie-dyed shirt. I had the realization I had not worn that shirt since the wreck. Where had my love of color gone? It died in the wreck. That made me very sad and I cried.

My homework for grief class was to list the myths about grief. At the top of my list was "I'm fine" followed by "I can't ask for help." I came to see the rest of my list had more excuses than myths. Blaming the trauma, feeling tarnished, and losing everything, including my self-confidence. Those feelings had been triggered by this new ten-week course. Where will this journey lead me?

We kept exploring the myths of grief and moved into the subject of what others had to say about our predicaments. Phrases like "it will get better with time," and "keep busy," and "you have to be strong for everyone else." Silly isn't it? When we know someone is grieving, we don't realize that no words will help. We feel obligated to say something and think that saying something may make us feel better, as if we could take the sting out of their grief with a snap of the fingers. Now, when a friend is grieving, I am able to say, "I know there are no words that will help you with your grief. I love you. I am here if you need me." I don't know if that helps them. I do understand their lives have been forever changed. Now it was my turn to wrestle with all those emotions stuffed down for years since the wreck.

I had one more week left in the chronic class. I made it through back-to-back classes, two days in a row for two weeks. Driving still overwhelmed me. I kept pushing through because I had to be fine. I kept saying to myself, "you can do this," and I did. I'm pretty sure that having to be okay was more exhausting than admitting I was hurt.

When the chronic class ended, it was both sad and happy, like the end of summer camp. I had bonded intimately with this new group, but I knew lunch dates would never be arranged. We were each there for our own agendas. We had lives to live and new things in our tool boxes to help support us, moving farther away from just surviving and closer to thriving.

There were still eight weeks of the grief class left, and thankfully, it was closer to home. Mom could see how much the weekly drive was wearing me down. I remember one evening a few years ago when I was staying with her, she studied me and said, "That wreck aged you ten years."

"I know. I wish other people would get that. I am sick of hearing "well at your age." Stop blaming my age. That really ticks me off!"

Finally home after six weeks of driving back and forth, I slept for two days. I only had one class a week now and was determined to complete the grief class. I didn't always like the way it made me feel. I didn't like facing my raw, pent-up emotions, but I knew it was helping and I knew I had to keep going. God bless Mom and Jack. I don't know how they put up with me, not being my real self for so long.

The grief class kept scraping away the layers of armor I had built up. We moved into an exercise looking at how we were rationalizing situations and what people tell us to help us with our problems. People would say, "I know how you feel, when I had a wreck..." and they would ramble on. All I could hear was blah, blah, blah. I didn't care about *their* wreck! This was *my* wreck, and it is unlike any other I have heard yet, and I tell you, I've heard a LOT of stories. Front ended, rear ended, t-boned, side swiped, but not one story where they were sent spinning like a top. I had empathy for their situations. I just didn't want to hear their stories. I was sick and tired of hearing them. I never got to tell my story because they were so busy jabbering on about theirs!

Other people have to share their stories, don't they? A young friend I worked with many years ago was about six months pregnant. It was her first time. She took her break, and when she came back, she was in tears. I asked what was going on and she told me everyone had to share their horror stories of childbirth. I told her to stop listening to them. "Picture your birth smooth, calm and tranquil. Did anyone out there tell you a good story?"

"No," she said through tears.

"Well I have one for you. My sister had her first baby in an hour or two. Her second one popped out in no time. So stop believing all those stories and know that your birthing experience can be so much different than theirs." She blew her nose, wiped her eyes and came over to my cubicle. "Can I have a hug?"

"Absolutely, anytime! Don't listen to those stories. I am here anytime you need me." I remember her laughter when I talked to her baby. She started to talk to it too. Her birth took under three hours, no problems, and no complications. When she came in a few weeks later to show off her new baby, I softly said "hi" and the baby looked directly at me.

"He knows your voice!" she gasped. We both smiled.

"I told you he could hear us." She kept smiling

"Thanks for everything! I am so glad you were around for me."

"Happy to help, love." Now that's a happy story.

Why don't we hear more of these happy stories? People hold on so tightly to their wounds, for fear of being lost without them.

The grief class was really kicking my butt. It truly made me face all I had lost in the wreck. The group was wonderful and supportive. I didn't know I needed to grieve. I didn't know you can't heal emotions with intellect. Every week more armor fell away and I felt the raw emotions of the grief.

Another assignment was to identify the short-term relief we relied on. I'd get angry and yell at people who aren't in the room. I'd yell at doctors, insurance people, anybody I could think of. I would work myself into an angry tizzy. I would isolate myself in the bedroom, my cave. I would grumble a lot, I would warn Jack, "I'm in a bad mood, it's got nothing to do with you."

He would always look at me and say, "Thanks for letting me know."

I would crawl back up the stairs, turn on the TV, pull the covers up, and hide in my cave. Another short-term relief that always ended badly was overdoing things when I felt good; completely exhausting my energy reserves. Then I would spend days in bed recuperating; another way to disconnect from the world. As long as I was hiding in my bedroom, no one would see me, and as long as I was worrying, I was doing something.

Somehow I managed to do my homework every week, and although it made me grouchy, it helped immensely. The homework was deeper and harder each week. The next assignment was to plot a graph of the good things and bad things in my life. Start with a straight line across and add events like a timeline. Above the line meant it was good and below the line was bad. Each line was labeled and the intensity of each was shown by how long the line was. We were asked to have at least two on top and two on bottom to help even things out. We each needed to look at our past and this helped us to not just see all good things or all bad things.

I was triggered by this exercise as I worked on my graph for days. It was gut- wrenching to look back at all the things I had been through. It was a miracle I was still here on this Earth. God must have a plan for me. Perhaps it's this book, who knows?

Working on the line graph helped me put my wreck experience into better proportion with the rest of my life. It could not undo what had happened to me, however, it made me realize how many times in my life I ran away to avoid grieving a situation. It was a tough week. When my graph was done, I outlined it on the computer, which actually gave me a greater sense of accomplishment.

After the graph exercise and sharing in groups, we were ready to move into the recovery stages of grief. All through class, the only thing required of us was to be honest with ourselves. Working from the graphs, we moved into working on apologies for things we had done, and forgiveness for those we thought had messed up our lives.

Throughout this recovery process, we wrote letters to people that would never be mailed. It was a way to express how we truly felt. This was another difficult assignment about letting go of the pain of the experience, as well as all the unfinished emotional garbage attached. We had two weeks to write the letters and then came the day to read them in class. When I read my letter, it was overwhelming. All the feelings that were in this writing came gushing out as I read. Tissue boxes slid across the table. After all the pain that came from working on the letter, I have to admit I felt better after reading it out loud.

We had completed our journey together. Our last group was a potluck celebration. We had unearthed our demons and dealt with our catastrophes. We had new tools to deal with our grief. It seemed easier to do the process guided by a facilitator who knew her stuff. She was very wise and always seemed to know what to say, no matter the circumstance. She was proud of all of us for sticking with it and making it through to the end. So was I. Exhausting as is was to dig up and deal with all the buried emotions, it was well worth the effort and is an experience I will never forget. I hugged the facilitator and thanked her for all her help and support. I told her she was an amazing woman and she responded back in kind.

For decades the word grief always seemed to include death. I thought I would feel so out of place because I was not grieving the death of a loved one. That is what usually comes to mind when I hear the word grief. From the very first day the group welcomed me with open arms and for that I will always be truly grateful. I came to realize I was grieving a death; it was my own death. It was the death of all the things I would never do again. It was a death of how I lived, and the death of the person I was before the wreck.

After all these years I was finally admitting and accepting how different my life became after the wreck. I used to be the fiery girl that bounced around the room; the loud one. Now I was the quiet girl suffering in the corner who got up to stretch quietly in the back of the room.

That was then and this is now. I had come a long way and learned a lot in those two months. I knew I had to be present in my own life or I wouldn't thrive. My situation was what it was and it was my choice as to what it would become. I had no desire to live from anger any longer. I wanted to be happy again and have my life back. I could have it all; it just looked different now.

"Enjoy present pleasures in such a way as not to injure future ones."

~ Seneca (ca. 4 BC — AD 65)

Chapter 29

Embracing the Inner Tortoise

With the chronic issue and grief classes completed, I felt I finally had time to let go and integrate all I had learned and experienced. It was time to embrace my "Inner Tortoise."

For years Jack has always told me to "slow down Honey," and many times he referred to me as the girl who wants it "yesterday." It was never really a problem before the wreck. I had plenty of stamina and energy and could go, go, go for days. The chronic issue class made me come face to face with reality. It forced me to face the fact that I could no longer run at my old pace. The weekly goal sheets in class made a difference. At first, writing them made me really cranky. It was more proof that my poor body couldn't do what it could before the wreck. One day in class I had the epiphany that I had picked weeds for fifteen minutes. It didn't sound like much until I remembered that five years ago I couldn't even remain upright for fifteen minutes.

I do try to pay attention to my limits, but some days I actually feel good and forget that I had a wreck. I know I will never get to use my tiller again. I hope to someday be able to use the weed-eater again, but it emits a lot of vibration. I was chatting with my Dad one day and told him that and he said, "Why would you ever want to use a weed-eater?"

"It's instant gratification; the weed is there and then it's gone. It gives me a sense of accomplishment." Dad chuckled. It's the same with mowing the lawn or using a tiller. I miss playing in the yard. For a long time I avoided the yard because I couldn't stick to my limits and I would hurt myself. Reframed after my classes, it's about taking the big goals and breaking them into smaller goals. What used to take me a day now takes two or three weeks. Sometimes it's very frustrating.

I still have to watch it when I exercise. I had always been as strong as a mule. In the chronic issue class I learned about my boundaries and my limitations. Some days I would feel really good, overdo it, and then I would be in bed for a week and would have to start all over again to get to step one. That's certainly good for making you feel like a failure and is most depressing. Setting weekly goals, like exercising three times a week for ten minutes, could be enough. After a few weeks, I could move that up to fifteen minutes. My biggest problem was being in a hurry trying to do it all in the same way I did before. Now I have come face to face with my Inner Tortoise and I must embrace it.

Another epiphany…any physical activity is action. I was stuck thinking I couldn't do anything, when actually anything I did with my body *was* action. When I repotted a plant, I was in action. Walking across the yard is an action. I had forgotten the basics. Any movement is action. I did do physical activity; I just needed to rename it "action."

I decided to make goal sheets for the summer. I took inventory of the garden to see what needed to be done. I had a small container garden since the wreck because that's all Dr. Gallo would allow me to have. Those plants had grown up over the last six years and really needed to be split. I think it took me all summer and lots of help to get it all done. Before, it would have taken a week, but now, splitting one plant a week is a struggle.

Splitting up the larger plants could put me in bed for a week and send me back to step one again. I started using a timer and did my best to pay attention to it and take breaks.

One day, during a break, a hummingbird flew into my little garden. He stopped for a drink and then sniffed a few flowers. When he was done, he hovered in the air staring straight at me as if to say "hello." His scarlet coloring was magnificent and watching him hover was amazing. After a minute of connection, he flew over my head and was gone. Had I been at my previous "run me ragged" pace, I would have missed it. I was learning how to find joy again and amazement in the little successes. Learning how to slow down and pace myself is actually a big success, although it tends to come and go. That summer, I did my best to honor my Inner Tortoise and kept chugging along at a slow pace. As Jack says, "those plants aren't going anywhere." By fall all of the plants but two were split.

I can't say I always behaved. Most times I didn't know I overdid it until an hour or two later, when the aches set it. That always confused me. How was I supposed to know to stop when it didn't hurt? I know it confused most of the doctors too. I think there are still fascia problems and maybe always will be. How do you crinkle up aluminum foil and get it all straightened out again?

Once, during a massage, I told Katy that no one could figure out what was going on, so I made up a new name. I decided I had "fractured fascia."

She smiled and responded, "You can't have fractured fascia because there's no bone in fascia. Bones fracture honey, not fascia."

I heard her. I knew bones fractured, but I decided I had the right to name it since no one else had figured it out. That would explain the time lapse between the action and the pain. Then again, what do I know? I'm just the patient that had run out of patience with being a patient, still getting bills and no answers.

Odd, it wasn't until I started the grief class that I realized I had something to grieve. All the years I spent trying to be tough and trying to prove I was okay were painful and exhausting. Both classes provided a safe environment in which I could learn about the death of my old life and the birthing of my new life. Who will I be now? I knew I must embrace my Inner Tortoise.

A few of my friends drove me crazy; always blaming my age. It made me furious. I knew what I could and couldn't do before the wreck. I taught classes in voice and movement and knew my body quite well. I lost it all in the blink of an eye because someone charged out of a parking lot and crashed into me.

All the craziness; all the lawyers with their smoke and mirrors. For a time I was lost in self-doubt. I remember one time at Mom's I asked her if I was making all this up. She reassured me it was real. "I have seen the difference. It's all real, Wendy, and you're not making this up." I flashed back to when Mom told me the wreck had aged me ten years and it was time to accept I would never get those years back.

Now I had to blossom into a new life that moved slower. Accept my new life and accomplish what I could get done by the doing. Use my timer, take my breaks, be gentle with myself, and speak kindly to myself in the mirror. I was very fortunate to be alive and upright after the wreck. I was still in the dark about where my new life would take me, but always glad I knew for sure that I had people who loved me. It helped a lot.

This time the race goes to the tortoise.

"Yield not to calamity, but face her boldly."
~ Virgil (70 BC – 19 BC)

Chapter 30

Deposition – the New Inquisition

After two and a half years in the medical circus, and now another three years invested with all the legal trauma drama, I was frazzled! I believe the insurance companies try to wear you down until you've got no fight left and are willing to walk away, settling for pennies.

I liked my new lawyer, Kit. He didn't make me get up for all those early morning case management conferences like Artie did. After the first eleven case management conferences, I was convinced that it was code for reschedule. I was so tired of the other lawyers; all those times I met Artie at the courthouse. Every time he told the judge that the woman who hit me had moved out of the country to Aruba, all the lawyers would laugh and offer to go down south and take her deposition. To them it was funny. To me it was cruel.

I remember the first notice I got from Kit, when the next case management conference had to be rescheduled again. I called to ask what time he wanted me to be there.

"There is no reason for you to be there. I will let you know what happens."

"Are you sure?"

"The judge will be scheduling another court date. There's no reason for you to be there."

"Okay then, I will stay home. Thank you, Kit."

"Don't worry, I have this covered. It will only be five minutes." His calm voice was reassuring. After each court date, I received correspondence by mail that usually arrived the next day. Kit always kept me informed of what was going on. I was glad not to go to the early morning courthouse meetings. There were occasions when it might have been easier for me to go, just to know what happened so I could relax.

Some days I called and spoke with Sally, his paralegal, to find out what happened that day. Sally was a lot like Tracy and another blessing along my journey. She had great people skills and knew how to soothe the weary human who had been turned into a blubbering maniac by the system.

Tracy told me a long time ago, "If you need an answer, talk with his paralegal." I was fortunate to work with paralegals that had an understanding and empathetic compassion for what I was going through. They were veterans of insurance battles and legal games.

The court rescheduled a continuance for another year and then we finally got some action. I received notice from Kit that my deposition had been scheduled. He also sent the defendant's opening interrogatories, which is fancy talk for a questionnaire. There were eleven pages of questions, an authorization for employment records, a notice to provide information of any Medicare payments made for medical services, a request for my tax returns, and an authorization to release all of my medical records to her insurance company.

Seven months later I received another set of interrogatives from my own insurance company. It was all part of the "dog and pony show." We finally got the information on her insurance policy; the limit was only $50,000. It made no sense to me. If her insurance policy only covered $50,000, why were both our insurance companies spending money on lawyers?

The never-ending questions, feeling beat down by the system, and I have to keep proving that I'm broken. It's humiliating and makes it very hard to heal. They are driving me crazy and milking the insurance companies. I have a whole new respect for lawyers; not the ones that attack people for insurance companies, but for the ones who work for people like me."

Do you know how your premiums are spent by insurance companies? In my state, auto liability insurance is required by law. I've paid premiums to the same company for over thirty years. Now I have a wreck and they spend money on lawyers instead of paying my settlement. It appeared her insurance company also preferred lawyers to paying a settlement. Lawyers who work for the insurance companies can do anything for a billable hour…a phone call, send a fax, write up notes…it's all billable. Their job seems to be to get out of paying the claim all-together or minimize any settlement. It's a cruel way to make a living. I know there are fakers who take advantage of the system, but I am not one of them. It would be way too much work! My medical bills were over $30,000 and her insurance company wants to settle for $6,500? I don't think so.

My lawyer said to me, "We are finally making good progress. All the right players are in place now, so we can get something done. The woman who hit you finally contacted her insurance company so we are good to go."

For those that are unfamiliar with all this legal stuff, a deposition is basically a question-and-answer session. Kit had to be the one who would finally get this all taken care of so I could get my check, right? The third time's a charm. He knew personal injury cases; it was all his firm did. My life was forever changed and even now, almost eight years later, I still work on accepting who I am today.

Kit had me come to his office the day before the deposition to prepare me. Jack drove us downtown; the parking lot was under the building. We actually found a parking place on the very first try. The stagnant smell of exhaust fumes hung heavy in the air.

We went to the elevator and pushed the "lobby" button. From the lobby we walked across the building to a different bank of elevators to go to the offices. Walking into my lawyer's office was intimidating even though I had been here before and the people were really nice. The deposition and all the legal pressure made me feel very small.

The receptionist at the front desk greeted us by name and said, "We have a DVD for you to watch which will explain the deposition process. Your lawyer will be in after you have watched the DVD."

We watched the DVD, which made some very good points, such as don't volunteer information, only answer the questions you are asked, and especially, don't let your emotions run off with you. Don't get angry, don't lose your temper, always remain calm. I took notes as we watched. While we were waiting for the lawyer, I had to stretch. Between the drive downtown and sitting to watch the movie, my body was grumbling in pain. I didn't want to take any meds before I came in. I was afraid I would miss something, do something, or say the wrong thing.

Kit came in and sat across the table from us. "Hi Wendy, hi Jack, did you watch the whole DVD?"

"Yes." I answered.

"Any questions?"

"No, not at the moment" I answered.

Kit turned very serious and looked right at me. "You need to know that during the deposition, they will be checking you out to see what kind of witness you would make on the stand. Try not to let them fluster or upset you and let me know if you need to take a break. If you don't know the answer, just say you don't know the answer. Don't tell any lies. I can work with the truth, but if you lie in a deposition, we could be screwed. We have all the right people involved now and I hope we can get this settled soon."

"Can Jack come with me?"

"It's not very common, but I suppose he could if he really wants to be there. I'll check with the other parties."

I thought I was prepared for the deposition. The trick now would be to stay calm through tonight and tomorrow. I was so glad Jack was driving. My mind was in that panic place where every car on the road felt like a threat. I could feel the adrenaline racing through my body.

We stopped at a red light. I took some deep breaths; it felt as though I hadn't taken a breath the whole time we were at the lawyer's office. The light turned green, Jack slowly started forward and a white car from the other direction started to turn right into us. Jack laid on the horn and I panicked. The woman looked up and slammed on her brakes, all the while on her cell phone. People can be so stupid. Why is common sense so uncommon?

My chest was heavy, breathing was difficult, and yet we were fine and nothing actually hurt me. I had a flashback of the wreck when that woman slammed into me and spun me like a top. I was freaked out by every car. I couldn't breathe and reached for my meds. I hadn't had any today because I wanted to be clear-headed. I felt like a deer in the headlights. I thanked God she didn't hit us.

Jack expressed his anger with the horn and some choice words but relaxed a few blocks later. Stuck in panic mode, I was exhausted when we finally made it home. It amazes me how much energy I use up when I'm freaked out and tensed up. I took my meds and lay down with ice packs, holding back fearful tears, hiding under the covers, my busy brain driving me crazy. "What will really happen tomorrow in the deposition?" "Will they attack me?" I had years to prepare for this day, and now that it's finally here, it scares the hell out of me. Many lawyers are called sharks after all.

I started wondering if it was a good idea for Jack to come to the deposition. I knew he wouldn't be allowed to say anything, and if he was in the room I knew I would keep looking at him, which would make me look more nervous. When I came downstairs later, Jack asked, "Do you really think it's a good idea for me to go tomorrow?"

"I've been thinking about that too. You know I love you, but maybe it's not a good idea after all."

"I agree. It's not too far from here, so I can take you and pick you up."

"That's what I was thinking too." Jack gave me a gentle hug and then I grabbed something to eat with my evening meds and tried to get some sleep, though it did not come easily.

I was worried about the deposition. I thought it would go quickly and we would be done in an hour or two. I didn't know there would be so much to talk about when there wasn't that much to talk about. She hit me, spun my car in circles, screwed me up for life, and then left the country before everything was settled. My mind was spinning, but in the wee hours I finally drifted off.

I awoke early. I needed to eat something before the deposition at 11:00. Fortunately, it was scheduled at her lawyer's office which was much closer to home, so there was no downtown traffic for us to deal with. Let the lawyers deal with it.

When we arrived at her office, we pulled in right behind Kit. I gave Jack a kiss and headed off with my lawyer. We chatted for a few minutes before going into the office.

"Remember," he said, "they will be watching every move you make. They will be sizing you up to see how you will do in court. Do your best to stay calm."

We went inside; the office was very relaxed and homey. I was nervous and shaky, but at least the surroundings felt comfortable. We were escorted into the meeting room, shown where to sit, and were told "cold bottled water is on the table and the bathrooms are down the hall. We are still waiting for the other lawyers, so please, make yourselves comfortable."

The court reporter was setting up her stenography machine. It was very small and looked like a black adding machine with unmarked keys. She was sitting on one end of the table to my left. My lawyer sat on my right. The other lawyer had laid her files directly across from me. I went to the bathroom and looked at myself in the mirror. "You can do this. You can do this!" I was trying to feel a spark of power but felt defeated before we even started. I went back to the conference room, grabbed a bottle of water, and sat down. My guts felt as scrambled as they did on the day of the wreck. We waited until the other lawyers had finally shown up. I wonder if they charge extra for being late.

They were dressed in expensive suits. I was sure these lawyers billed by the hour and, once again, the thought crossed my mind, "Why don't they just pay the settlement instead of paying lawyers." I was baffled. Why did they need all the legal trauma drama? The two new lawyers were getting oriented and found their seats at the opposite end of the table across from the court reporter. They laid briefcases and files on the table and all their tablets and pens, as they got ready to start. I think that was to mess with my mind; an emotional dig before we started. My own insurance company is paying for these lawyers out of my premiums? So, if they send two lawyers, do they double the bill? There was no question who was responsible for the wreck. Now the fight was over how much my injuries were worth. Her lawyer's job was to protect the insurance company's money so they don't have to pay anything, or at the least pennies to the dollar. My lawyer was the only one who didn't get paid by the hour and he was the only one in the room on my side.

All the lawyers made nice to each other before the deposition began. The lawyers chatted for a bit…"How are you," "How are the kids," "How was the vacation?" It was obvious they were acquaintances, although the feel of competition hung quietly in the air. One of her lawyers cracked a joke about going to Aruba to interview the woman who hit me in person. He thought it was a nice time of year to go south. He and his partner chuckled. I threw him a glance and remarked, "It would be nice to be able to actually travel again," and that shut him up. He actually looked at me with a glimpse of compassion. Perhaps for the first time he realized all the crap I had gone through to get to this stage in the game.

I was shocked when one of the lawyers said, "If my deposition doesn't last at least three hours, my boss will chew me out." I couldn't believe it. She had to make the deposition last three hours, even if it only took one? It sounded like another misuse of my premium money.

After that remark, my lawyer looked at me and winked. He quietly said, "Do your best to stay calm. They will try to rattle you."

"I'll do my best." I had watched the DVD and chatted with my lawyer the day before but I still wasn't sure how all of this was going to turn out.

"Wendy, when you need a break, make sure you tell me." Well, hindsight being 20/20, it would have worked out much better if I had told him that we needed to take a break every thirty minutes, because I did need a break at least every thirty minutes.

When everyone was settled, the court reporter swore me in. "Raise your right hand please. Do you swear to tell the truth, the whole truth, and nothing but the truth?"

"Yes," I said and the party started.

The lawyer sitting across from me was civil and tried to put me at ease. "We aren't trying to catch you up or anything." Wow, great start for putting all my defenses on high alert. "We need you to answer some questions. This isn't the Inquisition. When you need a break please say so." I bit my lip to stop from laughing. Of course it's an inquisition. That's why you are sitting directly across from me; the better to read my reactions.

She started off with my name and had me verify the interrogatory she had was the one I had filled out. "When you reviewed those, did you notice whether or not there was anything that needed to be changed or updated or supplemented?"

"Yes. It's missing the hospital where I went to the emergency room."

She asked about the hospital three different ways. I was tired of the same question being turned into another one.

I answered "uh-huh" to one of her questions.

My lawyer spoke up, "Is that a yes? You can't just nod your head. You have to either say yes or no."

After I answered the question verbally she said, "Thank you. Anytime you answer with anything other than a yes or no to a question that asks for a yes or no, someone, hopefully, will remind you to answer it verbally so she can get it done accurately. We're not trying to be rude. We're just trying to get a clear record."

She went over my education all the way back to high school. Why? She asked about the job I had been doing at the time of the wreck and another position with the same company I worked as a temp after the wreck for six months.

"Why haven't you worked since?"

"I can't sit and do a desk any longer."

"When you worked as a temp did that require you to sit at a desk?"

"Yes."

"How many hours a day did you sit when working the

temporary job?"

"Maybe three."

"So at any one sitting, you would only sit about three hours at a time?"

"No, I was only sitting thirty minutes at a time. I could get up and stretch when I needed to in that position."

I was working at the same company I had been with when the wreck happened. Dr. Gallo and my physical therapist set a maximum of twelve hours a week. I only worked three days a week. I worked for two hours, and then went to lunch. After lunch, I would work for one or two more hours. I knew of no other place that would be so flexible. Even with such a small schedule, there were days when I had to call in because of the pain.

The lawyer had moved on, asking if I had applied for disability, to which I answered yes. She looked like the cat that swallowed the canary when I told her we were in the appeals process.

"So your application was denied?"

"Yes."

"Originally, and you are now in the process of appealing?"

"Yes."

She continued to go after the disability angle. She almost looked happy that I was denied. When she heard the judge had ordered a psychological evaluation, and it was a few days away, she almost foamed at the mouth. She went on about the who's and the where's and when's of the testing. After about fifteen minutes, when that had been exhausted, she went after my medications. I was taking an anxiety drug and pain meds, but only when I needed them. I wasn't taking anything every day yet. She went on and on with never ending questions. Asking the same question over and over, changing subjects then popping back to a question she had already asked three times. She asked about my memory issues. She wanted to know if my memory problems were like those my friends were having or were they different.

I stated, "I don't sit around with my friends talking about our memories."

We took a break. The court reporter stood up and took a good stretch. I still couldn't do that without back spasms. I asked her "How long can this last?"

"This is your first time at a deposition, isn't it?"

"What's left to ask questions about?"

"Honey, these can last for days. You're doing fine, just hang in there."

I headed to the bathroom. I stretched and rinsed my face with cool water. Then I gave myself a pep talk in the mirror. "You can do this, Wendy."

When break was over the lawyer across from me reminded me I was still under oath. Then she pulled out a picture and laid it on the table in front of me. "Does this look like your car?" I was stunned. I was speechless. It was the first picture I had seen of my car after the wreck. In her picture, the doors were taped up so you couldn't see all the gaps between the windows and the mangled door frames.

"Yes, that's my car but it looked a lot worse than that. There were gaping holes above the windows and the passenger seat had been pushed all the way across to the console."

That damage you cannot see from one picture of the outside of the car. I have no doubt that they took this picture at the best possible angle that would make the car look best for their case. We had been in the settlement process for almost four years. The picture really rattled me and she knew it. She asked question after question and finally offered to take a break. Silly of me to think we only had five or ten minutes to go. I stood and began doing stretches facing the wall. I said, "I'm okay, let's get this finished." I was sinking fast and knew if I had to be there much longer, I would crack up.

When noon finally rolled around, one of the other lawyers said she needed to break for lunch. I was holding back the tears and asked Kit, "How much longer is this going to take?"

He gave me a subtle look and quietly said, "We'll talk in the hall." He knew I was on the verge of caving and didn't want the other lawyers to see me crack.

"I can't do this for two more hours. Yesterday I was upright for too long at your office, and today I'm about done."

He could tell I was distraught. He looked out the window, "Isn't that your husband out there?"

I looked out and said, "Yes, it is!" My heart jumped for joy. There was Jack sitting in the car. I went outside and told him we were getting ready to break for lunch, so don't leave yet.

Kit came out to the car and said, "Jack, give us five or ten more minutes and she can go. Let's go back inside." I cocked my head and looked at him over the car door.

Kit explained, "Instead of breaking for lunch when the first lawyer gets through, we will reschedule. She only has a couple of questions left and the other side would take the rest of the day today and..." he said looking straight at me..."I think you need to go home."

"No argument from me, I'm cooked!" I replied. I got a smooch from Jack and followed my lawyer back into the building.

We all reconvened in the conference room and took our seats. As Kit predicted, there were only a few questions left. When her questions were complete, Kit took the stage. "Instead of commencing after lunch, I suggest we find a day to reschedule and let them have their question time then."

I was trying to keep my cool and hold back my tears. I was done. I was spent for the day. The pain in my back was becoming unbearable; everything hurt. All I wanted to do was go home with Jack.

Everyone pulled out their date books to find a day when everyone was available. The first date mentioned was more than a month away, and in a very sarcastic tone I said, "How about tomorrow?" All of a sudden, they all found a date that worked for everyone only two weeks away. That worked for me; I wanted to get this over with.

They all marked their calendars. My lawyer turned to me and asked quietly, "Would you like to do this one at my office?"

"I would rather have it here. It's so much closer to home."

He said, "Okay, that works for me."

He informed the rest of the group that the next meeting would be in the same location. Once their calendars were marked and all their files zipped up, they started chatting and my lawyer turned to me and said, "You can leave now. You don't have to stay around for this stuff." Words I had been waiting to hear all day. I got my things together, said goodbye and thank you, and went to the car where Jack was waiting patiently.

When I got into the car I was already crying. Jack started to ask a question. I cut him off and frantically said, "Drive please, get me out of here!" So off we went my hero and me.

"I think you need meds."

"Yes I do! My body really hurts, and I've got the bowling ball and a thinking headache! This is a bunch of crap!" I reached for my pillbox with shaking hands. Once we were out of that neighborhood and I was breathing normally again, we decided on a drive-through place for lunch. I told Jack, "They just need to pay up. This is ridiculous, I know she paid her premiums, they said everything would be covered!" I was flabbergasted with the screwy system and shocked at how long they have gotten away with it.

By the time we got home, I was Little Miss Chatterbox. I probably didn't make a whole lot of sense, but Jack is very good at sitting there and listening while I go off on a million tangents. I suppose that's how I get rid of all the extra adrenaline; my tank was pretty high, even with all the pain. After venting for fifteen or twenty minutes and some lunch, I was calm enough to go lie down.

"Don't you think it's time for more pain pills? I want you to be able to stand up tomorrow." He handed me the pills and a glass of water and I followed his directions. Then Jack got me all fixed up with my pillows and my ice packs." If you need anything, you let me know. I mean it now…if you need anything, you let me know." He gave me a sweet kiss on the lips and then on my forehead. There's something magical about a loving kiss on the forehead when you feel dreadful.

When morning came I could barely stand up. No big surprise after such a busy week. I groaned all the way down the stairs and went straight for a hot shower. I'm glad the next deposition wasn't for two more weeks. I would be spending the next week horizontal with ice packs. And I suggested today for the other half? Holey Moley! That would have really sucked!

I received a copy of the deposition in the mail. It was traumatic reading through the pages, reliving the wreck, reliving the lawyers. It was overwhelming! It took me a few days, but I finally read through the pages twice, signed them, and got them in the mail back to Kit. One bright spot while reading through the deposition, I remembered the frustration in the lawyer's eyes when I answered the same question with the same answer, at least five times. Thanks to Mom and Dad for teaching me, no lying. When you tell the truth, your stories always match.

Same Deposition, Different Day

I checked in with my lawyer before the next deposition. He warned me they would throw a wide net trying to get anything they could get. I wish he had told me that the first time. Since I had done this before, I had a sense of what to expect, and somehow, that gave me some peace. I had done it before and I could do it again. Even with the prep work my lawyer did with me the last time, I felt blindsided and attacked, even though the lawyer was "playing nice."

The day for the rest of the deposition rolled around. Today I would be interrogated by the gal who said "if my deposition doesn't last at least three hours, my boss will chew me out." It worked out to my advantage for her to say that. She said three hours so I showed up expecting it to take four. I don't switch gears so well anymore. This time I would be ready.

We met at the same lawyer's office. We were on time and waiting for the other lawyers to show up, again. It still strikes me as odd that we were waiting for the lawyers who work for my insurance company. That seems so ridiculous. Why aren't they working for me?

This time my insurance company's lawyers were sitting across from me with all their piles and files on the table. The woman who would be asking the questions was directly across the table from me. The court reporter had me raise my right hand and swore me in before the testimony began. Interesting to think how much justice we would have if lawyers and judges had to be sworn in. Makes you think, doesn't it?

She started off very politely. "This is not a marathon. If you need a break, let me know." She would be asking questions, she wouldn't be trying to trip me up. This is supposed to be my time to tell my story, but in reality, this was the day when she got to attack me, and attack she did.

She started with questions I had already answered the last time. She quickly moved into "we have a diary that you kept from March 2004 through June of 2006." She grilled me about diaries and journals and calendars. I kept telling her I had no other diaries, journals, or calendars, but she kept asking for them.

Hindsight rears its head again. If I could go back, I would have told her "that's not a diary, those are notes you stripped out of my chiropractic file, so where's the rest of the file? Those notes go with the pictures in my medical file."

Next she asked about Jack's children, irrelevant time wasting questions. "Where do they live?" "What do they do for a living?"

I answered "I don't know."

She phrased it differently. "What do you think your husband's children would be doing for a living?"

"Objection, calls for speculation," said my lawyer. Right off the bat, she showed her true colors. This was the wide net I had been warned about. Three out of four lawyers in the room were there to protect insurance companies. I would love to see their bill!

Early on she asked, "Can we have an agreement? For the information that you don't recall, that if you do recall it later on, you'll let us know?"

"Yes."

I think she asked if I remembered that agreement a dozen times. I was so sick of her asking I started responding, "Yes, if I remember something I will respond through my lawyer."

Whenever she asked a question and I answered "I don't know," she always came back with, "do you have any documentation that you could reference to refresh your memory?"

My answer was always "no." She never looked too happy with me. Sometimes she would even rephrase the question, but the answer was still no.

She pulled out the police report and had me read over it. She wanted to make sure that everything was correct. It made me think she had an ulterior motive. Maybe something on the report would work in her favor. The copy she had was awful. I couldn't read the headings. She asked if there were any other parts I couldn't read and I replied, "I don't think so. There are a few discrepancies. We were not in a construction zone and it was not a clear day."

"So other than those two items, this report is accurate?"

"I think so."

She glanced a hateful look at me and in a snitty voice said, "If I give this back to you, can you *know* so?"

She went on grilling me. First it was information about my job, what I did and how much money I made. My disability claim was next on her list. She was anxious to get the report from the psych evaluation and was very disappointed when I told her I didn't have that information. She asked three times about that report. It was hard not to laugh at her and the way she was drawing everything out so she could get those three hours in.

She kept asking questions and I kept answering. Every now and then I would slide my hands under the table and rub my fingers, stretching them out. It's an easy modality anyone can do anywhere. Work your fingers one by one rubbing them from the base to the tip on all sides; give them a good massaging. You can also stretch the fingers gently backwards just so there's tension; you're not trying to break anything. If it hurts don't do it. The action of rubbing your fingers and stretching them out affects major acupuncture meridians, and the lower five chakras, moving stagnant energy in the body.

Now the lawyer had moved on to my "so-called" journal. It appears that, while none of the lawyers would use notes from my chiropractors; they were happy to strip out the notes I had written for the doctor each week. She asked me, "What does it mean here where it says your hip is cranky?"

"May I see the page please?" She flashed me a nasty glance and slid the piece of paper across the table to me. Too bad I wasn't thinking better. I would have asked her where the rest of the file was. Rather hypocritical to strip out what works from a medical file when they won't even treat chiropractors as a medical necessity or a valid expense when, in reality, those were two doctors that actually knew what they were doing. Ridiculous that insurance premiums were paying these people. There were other phrases she asked about and each time I asked to see the paper. She didn't seem to like this so every time she referred to one of those pages I asked to see it. She was taking everything out of context by using my notes and not my doctor's notes. Some of my notes don't make sense without seeing the page I filled out for the doctor each visit, which had diagrams I marked where the pain was and the pain level. There was a lot of information on those pages and they coincided with the paperwork she had stripped out of my file. So much for "the whole truth." I don't know how some people sleep at night.

The next round of questions was about the injuries I was "alleging" I suffered in the wreck. She went through each one slowly asking when I first knew there were problems with that area and "what helped you the most?"

"Atlas Orthogonal chiropractic, CranioSacral therapy, and massage." She threw me another nasty glance, I knew that wasn't the answer she expected but, in all truthfulness, those are the three techniques that helped me the most. Later down the road I would have injections for bursitis and more physical therapy.

Then she asked, "What has worked the best for your brain to heal?"

I looked straight in her eyes and said, "Time." I felt like I was getting her flustered and it felt really good. She buried her nose in her papers.

"I also used coloring books and taught myself to read and write again." She made a note and threw another glance.

She went through each doctor and asked when the last time was that I had seen them. I didn't know all those dates and I knew she already had the answers. I was growing impatient with her tactics to stretch the time of the deposition.

Every time we took a break, I went to the bathroom, washed my face, and had a talk with myself in the mirror. "You can do this. You can do this. Don't get cocky; just get it done." I was feeling much more confident than I did the first time. I was finally learning to play the game. If I had known that breaks were included in her three-hour time frame, I would've taken lots more. The comfortable chairs were uncomfortable after the first hour. Now the chair felt so hard; my butt was going numb.

She shuffled through her papers for about fifteen minutes looking flustered. The sarcastic me wanted to say "so, are we done yet?" but I behaved myself. She continued going over notes and shuffling papers until she found something. She slid another picture across the table and asked, "Is this your Facebook picture?" I was speechless. What does my Facebook picture have to do with getting crunched in the car wreck?

"Yes, I think that is what's up there."

"Do you know when this was taken?"

"I'm not sure, maybe Mom's birthday party." I felt blindsided and terribly confused. I actually have a day with my family and someone took a picture of me while I was smiling, is that supposed to prove I am fine and all healed up? I do remember she didn't ask if I was on any meds when that picture was taken, and I was. It felt like she was really reaching and having trouble making this deposition last for three hours.

I looked at my lawyer and saw his leg bouncing up and down under the table with impatience. He even looked a bit angry. He saw me hold up three fingers under the table, meaning this has to last three hours. I could see the subtle smile on his face.

The lawyer really looked like she was struggling to find a way to make this last. "I went out of order with my exhibit numbers so I'm entering an exhibit I didn't really intend to. Just so we're not confused on our record." She then presented me with printed pages from my website. "Is this the content of your website?"

"It appears to be. I am not certain what is actually out there right now, but these all look like pages I have had up." Another stunner, what does that have to do with anything?

On she went with, "Did you have this before the wreck?" "Did you have that before the wreck?" I could go on and on with the crap she asked but I think you get the idea. Be prepared for anything in a deposition. If you take meds, take them unless they make you stupid. They will use whatever they can dig up against you, anything to refute the claim, anything for a billable hour.

Finally she said, "I have no more questions for you." I looked at my lawyer and then at his watch. It was three hours on the nose. She got her three hours in. I just grinned at her. She asked my lawyer if we would accept the deposition as is or if I would read and sign off.

My lawyer was emphatic, "She will read them and sign off."

After the deposition you have the option to read the transcript or agree right then and there that they are fine. WARNING: Read them before you sign them! Read *everything* before you sign it! When you receive the deposition transcript, you have the right to read through it, and if there need to be changes you have that option. Once that is done, discuss any changes with your lawyer before you sign off and accept the deposition.

After all the legal stuff, my body was much worse than it had been for a long time. All the sitting and stress and rattled nerves tied me in knots. By the time the two-day deposition was over, my body was flared up everywhere and screaming for attention. I called Dr. Benson's office for an appointment.

When Dr. Benson came in he took one look at me and said, "You don't look too good, what have you been doing?"

"Lawyers and depositions; it's been horrible. Reading the deposition transcript is horrible. I have an anxiety attack on every page. It's awful. I read a little bit and cry a little bit, and then it is time to walk away. I wanted to call weeks ago, but I didn't want to show up at the deposition taking steroids."

"Yes, they can make you seem much better than you really are. Don't want to go in hopped up on steroids? That was probably a good idea." We chuckled. He took a few looks, sizing me up. "Well I know what's wrong with you. It's all the damn lawyers and the stress they are putting you through."

My eyes were already tearing. When I heard his words and the truth he spoke, I started to cry.

He continued with a twinge of anger in his voice, "Lawyers can be awful; they only slow your healing process. All that stress is eating at you, I can tell just by looking at you. You're trembling. You want to cry all the time, don't you?" My lip was quivering. "It's too much to deal with and overwhelm only makes it worse. Are you depressed? If you're not depressed, you're in denial." He handed me the tissue box, his voice softened. "You were in a terrible accident, it was bad. Don't let them talk you out of that. This really did happen. It's been years of treatment to get you to this stage. I don't want to see you beat up by lawyers and back-stepping to step one again. There is nothing else we can do medically but maintain what you have. Your body will never be the same. You will never be the same. Lawyers can set your healing back years. How long has the legal side taken?"

"The legal stuff has been going on for four years now."

"Four years," he drew out the words repeating me in a tone of outrage. "That's ridiculous! Your claim should have been paid years ago. With all this going on, it's no wonder you're feeling like this. This part can be worse than the actual wreck. Now, do you understand why I say if you're not depressed, you're in denial?"

"Yes" I said tears rolling down my cheek. He had brought up antidepressants before but I had always refused. This time I was ready. I didn't want to feel like this any longer. I was exhausted, whiny, and in general felt crappy most of the time. My spirit wasn't broken, but it was showing serious signs of cracks.

After checking me out, he gave me a couple of joint injections for the bursitis flares, and wrote out two new prescriptions. "One of these is for sleep and the other is an antidepressant, take it the mornings."

"Now that the depositions are done, maybe I can heal more," I said. One thing about having a car wreck with only soft-tissue injuries, you have to keep proving your body is broken. It's very difficult to heal with that conflict going on inside."

He handed me the prescriptions and said, "Let's give these a couple weeks and see how you feel. If you have any problems before then, call my office, okay?" I was holding the prescriptions in my hand and I sheepishly nodded yes. I was afraid if I said anything else I would burst out crying. Dr. Benson had been good to me. I trusted him, so I'd give the new pills a try.

He also gave me a refill on my anxiety meds and insisted, "Take these before reading any more of that deposition. All that does is traumatize you all over again. It makes you relive the wreck every time you are reading it. It also takes you back to the trauma of the deposition itself and how awful the lawyers and insurance companies have treated you."

It seems I can do wonders for my occasional client and yet I have so much difficulty helping myself. It's a huge inner conflict. One afternoon about three years after the wreck, Jack walked into my office and asked why I was still having problems with pain when I knew all this stuff. I had been thinking about the exact same thing for years. I turned around and quietly said, "I think you should leave the room now, thank you." It was very frustrating to not be fixed by now.

Within a month, the lawyers for the other insurance company sent out thirty-two subpoenas; three to people I have never even heard of. They already had the medical records. More wasted time and billable hours. I got three calls from very upset providers. The depositions never happened; the subpoenas were all quashed (dismissed) by the court. So, more billable hours to confirm with everyone the depositions had been canceled. Was there no end?

"Life becomes easier when you learn to accept an apology you never got."
~ Robert Brault (1938 -   )

Chapter 31

Mediation for Settlement

After my deposition, the next step was a court-ordered mediation. It was scheduled about two months before my trial date, which had been on the docket for a year.

During mediation, my lawyer and I were in one room and the other lawyers were in another room. The designated mediator went back and forth from between rooms trying to get us to agree on a number to get this case settled. We played the game, back and forth, all afternoon. I should have taken more anxiety meds; I was a mess the whole time. Just being there brought me to tears. The afternoon wore on and the numbers weren't getting any better. The mediator came back with an offer that did not include the chiropractor, CranioSacral, or massage bills. Hindsight rears its head again. I wish I had said "my insurance guy said that pain and suffering is usually twice the amount of the medical bills. So you owe us that amount times three, right?" They wouldn't budge from their number, so it was decided that nothing would be decided today. More billable hours; how lucky for them.

There was already a court date set. I'd gone this far, I could handle a day in court, maybe. Kit called to let me know that another offer had been made. We both thought it was too low.

"What do you think about going to court?" I asked.

I could almost hear Kit thinking on the phone.

"This is something to really look at. If we continue and go to trial, we will have to start paying experts and money goes really fast once that starts. You could go to court, spend all that money on experts, and could still wind up with nothing, even if you win."

"So what do you think?"

"If we do go to court, my biggest worry would be you. When we were in mediation, no one even asked you a question and you still couldn't keep it together. I don't know if you would make it through a court trial, Wendy. It can be quite brutal."

"Have you had others win in court?"

"I had one recently. My client said it was the worst thing he had ever been through in his life, but he said it was worth it because we got a large settlement. He also said he would probably never do it again. I am happy to do what you want to do, but I think we would be better off if we could get the settlement offer up a little higher and take it. Then this would all be done and you could really start to heal. Think about it for a couple days and let me know."

"Thanks Kit. I will talk with you soon."

I felt numb as I hung up the phone. Could it possibly be that the end was actually in sight? I started crying. Jack came into the room and I told him what Kit had said. We talked about it for a while and I still couldn't answer the question either way… settle or trial? Jack said, "It's up to you Honey; why don't you call your Mom for advice?

As soon as Jack said that, I immediately knew, "I need to call my Dad."

I went up front to the office, took a deep breath, and dialed Dad's phone number. I was trying to be strong and not weepy when Dad answered the phone.

"Hello?"

I could hear my voice cracking when I said, "Hi Dad, I need some advice."

"Sure, I'll help if I can."

"I have the choice to take a small settlement or I can go to court, which will cost a lot of money up front for experts. I don't know which one to do. I've been through four years of this legal crap. I'm afraid I won't live through the trial."

"Well, Honey, if you don't think you would live through a trial, then why put yourself through one?" he said rationally.

"That's a good point. I think if we go to trial I might get more money. Of course, a jury can go either way and I could walk away with nothing."

"So, I think you have your answer, don't you?" he said calmly.

"I guess so. That sounds like the right answer too. Thanks Dad."

I went back to the living room and told Jack what Dad said. Jack agreed. "Kit said he would call back in a few days and let me know what kind of numbers he got. I'm hoping for good ones. Wow, if it's really over, then what will I do?"

"Now maybe you will finally relax. When it's over, it's over

Wendy. You'll have to let it go. No shoulda, woulda, coulda's."

Wow, it hit me. I had been steeped in this medical circus and the legal loopholes for so long, I didn't know anything else. I didn't know if I could let it go.

Kit finally called with the offer and said he didn't think he could get any more out of them.

"Okay, let's get it done."

"Are you sure?"

"I don't think I would live through a trial. We'll do the settlement."

"All right, I'll make it happen. I should have a check for you in a week or two. I will let you know when you can come pick it up."

A week later Kit phoned. "I have your check ready. When would you like to come pick it up?"

"It's too late today; we'd never make it downtown by five. How about tomorrow around two?"

"Tomorrow at two, see you then, Wendy." It was surreal. Had we finally made it through the worm hole?

The next day Jack drove me downtown to Kit's office for the last time.

The receptionist went down the hall and reappeared again. "Kit is expecting you, just down the hall to your right." Jack and I headed down to his office. He had the check ready and the paperwork for me to sign. I signed by the arrow and Kit handed me a check. Forty percent plus expenses went to the lawyer. He had spoken with medical providers to lower the amounts due so the providers had to write off some bills. Then the medical liens for the chiropractors and my health insurance were paid off. I got what was left. I was hoping for twice as much but it is what it is. Sorry I can't share how much the settlement was, it's confidential.

I finally had the check in my hand. My heart was pounding. It was really over! We took the check to the bank and the circus was really over! All the legal loopholes and jumping rope were done, over, finished, Finito!

If you ever find yourself in this predicament, get the best personal injury lawyer you can. If the wreck happened today, I would probably have a lawyer within weeks. The contingency fee contracts I saw were pretty much the same: nothing up front; you might have to pay their expenses, win or lose; you pay thirty percent if settled and forty percent if a court date is set. A court date being set doesn't necessarily mean you will go to trial, but it's still forty percent. Each state is different so do your homework. Most personal injury lawyers are happy to give you a free consultation. If the lawyer doesn't think you have a case, they will tell you.

Now, back to the disability process and lawyer number four. It had been ages since I appealed and no word yet on a hearing date.

"A handful of patience is worth more than a bushel of brains."
~ Dutch Proverb

Chapter 32

Disability? Get Thee a Lawyer!

A year after filing my appeal for disability, I finally received the letter stating my disability hearing had been scheduled at the Office of Hearings Adjudication and Review (ODAR), located in the Social Security office downtown. After two years, we were finally getting somewhere.

I was still terrified of other drivers and the thought of driving downtown still really scared me. It was so overwhelming; I cried at the thought. Learning that the hearing was scheduled was almost as stressful as filling out all the paperwork. It was finally happening; I would get to speak to the judge and tell him my side, or so I thought.

Jack did the driving and I tried to keep my eyes off the road and away from the other drivers. We arrived a half an hour before the 1:00 hearing and were greeted by a security officer sitting behind the reception desk. He asked for our IDs, asked us to sign in, and then he came out from behind the desk waving a metal detector wand while we assumed the position.

"Do you really have that much trouble here?" I asked in disbelief.

"We've had a few that got pretty upset when benefits were

turned down. This is just a precaution ma'am, you should be fine," he said with a friendly smile.

When he finished our security check he pointed to the window across the lobby and said "Check in at the window over there. She'll help you. Good luck."

We proceeded to the window, signed in, and I was handed more paperwork to fill out, including another medical release and another copy of "The Paperwork Reduction Act". I thought it was odd that the paperwork reduction act used up so much paper! Every time I was mailed more forms, I would get another copy of the paperwork reduction act for each form I received, even if that meant three copies for one envelope. I flashed Jack the paper and we both laughed. I had been receiving these since filing in October 2008. I filled out the paperwork and returned it to the woman at the window.

"Have a seat and they will call your name when they're ready for you."

I went back and sat down next to Jack, rolling my eyes at the bureaucracy. After sitting for 20 minutes my back was cramping, so I walked around the lobby a few times and went to the bathroom. The bathroom was a nice, large room where I could do some serious stretching and not feel like an idiot when people stared at me. I was already spent and ready to go home by the time we heard our name called. It had been more than an hour.

The woman who called our name raised her hand so we could see her. We followed her into a small courtroom. She gestured to a chair against the wall for Jack and I found myself sitting in front of a microphone. My heart was in my throat and the tears were already coming.

The judge introduced himself and asked my name for the record.

"My name is Wendy Teague and I am here today for my hearing."

The judge replied "You will not have your hearing today. Today is a pre-hearing." I felt a bulge in my throat and the tears came flooding.

"I have been waiting for this hearing for two years, and now you tell me it's not my hearing date?" I sniffled. I glanced at Jack and our eyes met in disbelief. We waited for years for this day to come and we waited for over an hour to get in this room. I was outraged and in despair.

The judge looked straight at me and continued. "We are limited by what words we can use in our mailings; that's why it uses the word hearing. I have no control over that, and for that, I'm sorry. You have to realize we have a backlog of five thousand cases. As we move this case forward, I want you to collect any medical records that we don't have on file yet. Get yourself a lawyer."

I felt like a deer in the headlights. The judge was adamant. "Get yourself a lawyer. We are done here for today, Mrs. Teague."

The judge closed the file and moved onto to the next one, making it obvious we had been dismissed. I felt like I had been talking to the elusive Wizard of Oz. I wondered how big the back-log was when I appealed two years ago. I was mad and then I softened. I wouldn't want his job.

Jack and I left the small courtroom, walked through the waiting area, and bid the security agent a good day. Once we were outside, both of us could cut loose. Jack was angry and I felt crazy; we both used colorful language. To top it all off, they don't stamp the parking tickets so we walked to the hotel next door where they were more than happy to stamp it for us. We used the restroom and then walked back to the car. I was so confused I wasn't sure what to do. Now I need a disability lawyer...lawyer number four? My heart was racing and I felt a panic attack coming. I popped some pills before the panic had a chance to completely engulf me.

We were both upset on the drive home. I was so preoccupied with anger and confusion, I only freaked out once when I saw a large white pickup truck pulling out on our right side. I'd been hit on the right side and had become so skittish of people pulling into traffic, especially when they are on my right side, driving something big and white. It's a new reflex I haven't been able to break.

After a few days of recuperation, I remembered a friend whose husband had used a disability lawyer. I called and asked her for the information and boy she had a lot. I took notes and wrote down the phone number. When we were done chatting, I called the law office and made an appointment. The woman on the phone said she would be sending me a packet with the forms I needed to fill out and bring to my appointment.

I received the packet and filled out the paperwork. I was back to "hurry up and wait" again. Mom's voice rang in my head as it said "Patience Little Jackass." I had been hearing the word patience for so long and I was running out of it. It had been four years since the wreck, and at this point, I had no settlement, no disability, no paycheck, and I was too messed up to work. I had another meltdown over money. I knew how tight things were. I hoped that having a lawyer would speed up the process.

Jack came upstairs to check on me. He sat on the bed and looked at me. I started blubbering. "You should divorce me; you would be better off. I can't work; I've got no money coming in to pay bills. You should divorce me, you would be better off." I was drowning in tears.

He looked me in the eye and softly said, "How would I be better off?"

"You wouldn't have to deal with all of this anymore. Doctor bills and credit cards…I owe so much money! You would be better off without me!"

"I love you Honey. I'm not going anywhere." He folded his arms around me and held me while I cried buckets.

The day finally arrived for my appointment with my new disability lawyer. As usual, Jack drove. The trip took a good half-hour and I checked that I had all my information three times before we left. When we got to the office, I signed in and a few minutes later our name was called.

"Hello, I am Camille and will be taking your information today." We were led back into the bowels of the office. I thought our appointment was with the lawyer, but I guess not. She was the paralegal; very nice and sincere. I had made copies of all my paperwork for them. I also showed her the medical records I had.

"We don't need to worry about your medical records today; we will get those from Social Security." She looked at the pile of paperwork I brought with me. "So have you done all this work alone so far?" she said in a voice of shock.

"Yes."

"That's quite impressive. That's a lot of work to do all by yourself!"

"Yes it was a lot of work. It's been two years since I filed. Had I known better, I would have started with a lawyer and I have no doubt he would have answered the questions better like, problem is: PTSD, Costochondritis (the swelling in my rib), and pinched nerves sounds more effective than the way I put it: I had a car wreck, my back hurts and I can't sit up long." I got weepy and had promised myself I wouldn't. I was embarrassed. "So sorry to break down, it's been a long two years getting here."

"How long has it been since the actual wreck?"

"Almost eight years and it's still not settled. I've been trying to get the insurance settlement for about four years."(The deposition for the insurance settlement had not happened yet.)

She smiled. "Well, you don't need to worry about this, that's what we're here for. We'll take good care of you. You're doing just fine."

I had no doubt she had done this before. She was good with irrational people. I am grateful for great paralegals! They are the humanity in law.

"I will go through all this and make sure we have what we need and then we will set an appointment with the lawyer." We went through the information from the paperwork as she matched it with her computer. The appointment took less than an hour but it was still wearing on me. She pulled out one more piece of paper; it was their contract. I saw a look of surprise on her face as I started to read it.

"Don't people usually read this?" I asked her.

"You know, they usually don't."

It was only one page, so I kept reading. You know how lawyers advertise they're free if you don't win your case? Well that's not the whole truth. In the middle of the document there was a line that read, should they lose the case, I was still liable for their expenses. I looked up at Camille and said, "So here it says if we don't win I still owe you money. How do I know what this could cost me?"

"It wouldn't be more than $500."

"Well that's the problem, that's why I am filing for disability. I can't work and I don't have any money."

"I wouldn't worry about that," she said in a relaxed voice. "Should you not win your case, we can always work out a payment plan." I felt the panic rising inside but I was determined not to cry again. I took a deep breath, looked at Jack, and then signed the contract. I handed her the paper and leaned back in my chair and let out a big sigh. Then she handed me my parting gifts. I received a canvas bag full of information about services available locally and a T-shirt.

I asked her "If you keep the T-shirt and the bag do I save any money?"

"No dear, sorry," she said with a warm smile. "You'll be hearing from us soon, and remember, getting scheduled in court again may take anywhere from twelve to eighteen months, possibly longer." More "hurry up and wait," I thought to myself as I smiled back at her.

Once we were outside, I let out a huge sigh of relief as we walked to the car. "That wasn't so bad." There was a small crack in my voice but I was holding it together. Jack looked at me with a glint in his eye and I could hear him without him saying a word...Patience Little Jackass!

Within a week I received a welcome letter from the disability attorney's office. It explained how their office worked and who I should contact for information and updates. Once again, I was reminded how long it could take for this case to be determined. The phrase in the letter was "try and be patient." My inner jackass was laughing. I was so tired of people telling me to be patient. One more time and I might snap.

The introduction letter went on to outline what they expected of me and what I should expect of them. If anything changed, I was to let them know. If I received any documents directly from Social Security, I was to let them know. It reminded me again to be patient because it may require considerable time to prepare my case. Basically they said don't call us, we'll call you. I have learned that's how many lawyers work. I knew now that, if a lawyer was busy working on my case, I shouldn't interrupt.

Five weeks later I received a letter from the law firm scheduling my pre-hearing conference with the lawyer. I was stunned. My hearing with the judge had been scheduled two months out. I had a lawyer; it was his job to take care of me and it was my job to let him. The letter also included court etiquette and how to handle myself appropriately; all very good information.

I didn't know who my lawyer was yet. The conference was scheduled two weeks before the hearing and time seemed to be crawling. I was really nervous and uncomfortable when we went to the conference. Of course, there's always the possibility that I had become allergic to lawyers, this being the fourth one!

Bless Jack, who drove me out there again. When we arrived at the office, I signed in and the woman at the front desk twirled around with a warm, happy smile and said. "Hello. Wendy right? I will let him know you're here."

Jack and I sat down and within minutes a tall man was standing in the doorway.

"Hello, you must be Wendy. I'm Brad, your lawyer." We all shook hands then followed him down the hall to his office.

We all sat and he asked if there were any questions to start with. I had to speak up. "I received a letter for a hearing and when I got there, there was no hearing. It was a "pre-hearing" and the judge told me to get a lawyer." I was about to continue when I saw Brad start to smile, so I waited to hear what he was going to say.

"Yes, we refer to that as Rocket Docket day. The court wants to make sure that you'll show up before they schedule professionals and experts for the hearing."

"It would have been nice to know that. I sat so long waiting for my non—hearing that I hurt all over. It was a waste of time; two hours I think."

"That won't be the case this time. Your hearing is confirmed, we all have your medical records, and we're good to go." He went over the information I had been mailed to make sure I understood it all. He also asked for updates, if my condition had changed, what medications I was taking, and if I was seeing any new doctors.

He said, "We will be fine with what we have; no worries. I can't stress enough that you just be yourself at the hearing. Don't exaggerate anything, but don't minimize your problems either. If the judge asks you a question, you tell him the truth. What you're wearing now is fine. Don't get all dressed up. Be honest with the judge."

"So you think we have a chance?"

"If I didn't think you had a chance, we wouldn't be here," he said with a boyish grin and a twinkle in his eye. It was reassuring that he thought we had a case. We went over a few more guidelines and then we were complete.

"Your hearing is scheduled for 1:00. I want you to meet me there thirty minutes before the hearing. We'll have a small office for privacy and we'll go over all this again." He stood up, shook our hands and walked us back to the lobby. I felt supported and was assured he knew what he was doing. This firm only handled disability cases. The front bulletin board in the lobby was filled with thank you cards and letters and I felt I had a chance this time.

I received a notice that the judge had to reschedule. Okay, four more days of "hurry up and wait." I could make it four more days. Even with three weeks' notice, those four days were spent waiting for the other shoe to drop. It was nerve-racking. What if there is no wizard?

I felt like a cog in a really screwed up system. I am on my third lawyer for the insurance settlement. It was advantageous for the insurance lawyers that I was first denied disability. Now I have a lawyer for disability. It would help my settlement case if my disability finally went through, but the system doesn't work that fast.

The hearing date finally came and Jack drove us downtown to meet the lawyer prior to the disability hearing. We went through security and I signed in at the window. Again I was handed more paperwork and they wanted a list of anyone who would be accompanying me. I completed the paperwork and returned it to the window. I looked around for my lawyer, but didn't see him anywhere.

Several minutes later he walked over to us with a grin on his face. "I've never seen paperwork filled out like this before." He was referring to my list of people, I included his name. "I have never seen anyone list their lawyer before."

"It says to list everyone I brought with me and I figured that included you too."

We followed him across the lobby and down the hall to a small office on the left where we met before the hearing. He proceeded to explain how the court seating was set up. He explained an MD would give testimony and there would be a vocational expert there as well.

"What do these people have to do with me? I have never met them. The doctor isn't even from this state, how would he know what's going on?"

"The doctor has all of your records. His job is to be neutral and testify to the court his opinion of your condition. You need to know that I rarely cross-examine a doctor because the doctor usually wins. The vocational expert will testify what kind of jobs you are able to do with your injuries."

I could feel the overwhelm creeping in. I was still confused why a doctor from out of state would be testifying. It made no sense. I had never even met the man.

The lawyer continued. "When we get in there, you will be sitting in front of the microphone and I will be sitting to your right. The judge will talk a little bit and then we go first. I will ask you questions and you will answer them. Make sure you stay on point and answer the question I ask you. When we are complete, the judge will then question the doctor and, as I told you, I rarely cross-examine the doctor if it won't help our case. Once the doctor has completed his testimony, the judge will ask questions of the vocational expert. Stay calm and we'll be all right."

After all of the explanations, I felt a bit more settled about the process. He quickly ran through all the questions he had asked me when we met at his office to refresh my memory.

"Do you have any more questions before we go in?"

"Not that I can think of right now. They will probably all come up two minutes after I get in that room."

There was a knock at the door; they were ready for us. I took my seat, kept my mouth shut, and did my best not to cry. The judge was sitting at his pulpit and welcomed us to his court. He explained how everything would work and then asked

"Do you have any questions before we continue Mrs. Teague?"

"No."

The judge turned the proceedings over to my lawyer, who began asking the questions we had gone over. Once we were finished, the judge took control of the courtroom again. He got the doctor on the telephone. I was in shock, a doctor I had never met, who had never examined me was going to testify about me on the phone, but I kept my mouth shut, as directed. The judge asked the doctor to present his findings. The doctor began rambling using my own notes against me. I felt my anger brewing. From what I heard it seemed he was missing most of my medical records. Especially when he said I had been fine since September of 2004. I flashed a look at Jack; both of our mouths hung open in disbelief. I looked at my lawyer and he motioned for me to stay quiet.

After the doctor was done telling his story, the judge asked my lawyer if he had any questions, to which he answered "no." I was really ticked off but managed to keep my mouth shut. The judge thanked the doctor for his time and told him they would be talking in another hour and the call was ended.

Now the judge was looking at me as if he was studying a painting. "Well Mrs. Teague, I am somewhat in a quandary. The doctor is telling me you are fine and you are telling me something different." The judge looked at his computer screen and then flipped through some paperwork.

The judge addressed the court, "At this time, I am going to order a psychological exam for you. You will receive the information for your exam in the mail. Make sure you do not skip this appointment or your case will be denied. Good luck to you." We had been dismissed.

"Thank you Your Honor," my lawyer said as he gathered his papers up and put them in his briefcase.

He gave me a look and I said "thank you" and we left the room.

I was so mad, I thought I would explode. The lawyer led us into another conference room to calm me down. "That doctor doesn't even know me! A psych test? It's been eight years since the wreck and I still can't work so now I must be crazy?" I exclaimed though tears.

"Calm down. Calm down. The doctor stated his opinion, the two of you just don't agree, that's all."

I was so angry! I felt betrayed by someone I had never met. The tears were flowing.

"So now I'm just screwed?" I snarled.

"We don't know that. Take the exam and we will go from there. Look at the bright side, he didn't deny your claim. Hang in there a little bit longer. Remember, this process can take a long time."

Again? Really? "Hurry up and wait?" I looked at Jack and knew he was steaming too. The lawyer waved at his next client. We said our goodbyes and got the hell out of there. Once again, we walked to the hotel next door to get our parking ticket stamped, headed for the car, and then home.

It only took two weeks to receive the official letter from disability scheduling my psych evaluation. The appointment was for the end of the month at 9:00 on a Saturday morning. I felt the lump in my throat. That would be only a few days after the first deposition for the insurance settlement. So, once again it was "hurry up and wait." I was freaked out the entire month. At least this time, a local doctor would be seeing me in person, not a strange voice spouting on the telephone. The letter also included what I should and shouldn't bring and to arrive fifteen minutes early. I had to sign a paper confirming I would keep the appointment for the court. There was also a notice that a copy of the report would to be sent to my lawyer.

After returning that paperwork, I received still more paperwork directly from the doctor that would be doing my evaluation. This form included all the information that was already in my records. The top portion asked for my current address, present illnesses, childhood illnesses, and my educational background. It went on to ask if I had ever been in prison, jail, a halfway house, drug treatment, alcohol treatment, or a psychiatric hospital. At this point, I thought for sure they were trying to drive me crazy so insurance wouldn't have to pay a thing because it was all in my head.

It asked for my most recent work history, any medications and the reason for taking them, plus a description of my daily activities. At this time I could only be upright for a couple hours and then I had to lie down most of the day. I was only able to sit at my desk for thirty minutes at a time. I tried to get some sun each day for twenty to thirty minutes when it wasn't too hot. I used ice when I needed it and was usually lying down by seven in the evening. Pretty boring lifestyle, considering I had been such a vibrant person before the wreck.

I did my best while I waited for the exam. I didn't want to be seen as a woman on the edge. I realized what a good point my lawyer had when he said the judge didn't refuse my benefits. When the day finally came, Jack drove me to Midtown for the exam. I had been in knots for weeks and felt like a pretzel. So where's the chocolate coating?

After a few minutes the doctor came out of his office. "Hello, I am Dr. James."

"Hi, I am Wendy and this is Jack."

"And what is your relationship?"

"We're married."

The doctor looked as Jack and said, "The test shouldn't take more than an hour." We knew that was code for "Jack can't come with you." I kissed Jack and he headed to the car.

The doctor walked me into his office. The anxiety had been building for weeks. I could feel my whole body trembling. I wouldn't last much longer. I freaked out thinking that, if I didn't pass this test, they could lock me up in the nuthouse. The doctor spoke for a few minutes in a very calming voice. He asked me simple questions I had already answered on his form.

"You seem very anxious" the doctor said watching my hands tremble.

"I am, I had a car wreck, the insurance company won't settle, I'm trying to get disability and now they think I'm crazy."

"No one has said you're crazy." The tears were streaming down my face and the doctor handed me a box of tissues. "Take a minute to collect yourself while I speak with another patient. I will return in a few minutes."

The doctor left his office and spoke with someone in the waiting room. I was still shaking, but the tears were slowing when he returned to the office.

"So, tell me what has you so upset?"

"I was in a car wreck six years ago. My body is broken, and no one who was supposed to help is helping. I haven't worked since the wreck, so money is really tight."

"So, you are feeling anxious and worried that you are not making money?"

"Yes! And the doctor bills keep coming!" The tears were flowing once again.

"Everything is all right. We will do two simple exams today. The first one is very quick and we will start on that one now." The first exam was for my memory using flashcards. He would show them to me, and after a bit, ask me what the card was. I never understood how that type of memory test worked. I suppose it showed my short-term memory was doing fine.

"For the next test I will have you work in a room across the hall." I followed him and took my seat in the small cubicle.

It was a psychology test where you filled in the circles with a number-two pencil. It reminded me of being in high school. He also oriented me to the building, "The bathroom is off to the left of the lobby, here is a key for you. It is fine to take a break anytime you need to. You can go outside as well. I will be in my office with another patient. If you have any questions, write them down. I will be back to check on you and answer any questions you may have."

The test booklet was overwhelming. I don't remember how many hundreds of questions there were, but there were a lot. I cried for a few minutes and then convinced myself that I could do this. I opened the book and began reading the questions. I had a separate sheet of paper where I wrote down questions for the doctor. He came in after about thirty minutes to check on me. I had more questions than I had dots on the answer sheet. What used to be simple questions were so hard now.

For example, I asked the doctor, "How do I answer a question like 'Do you like to travel?' when I used to travel and I like to travel, but now I can't travel?"

"Answer the questions with the abilities you have now," he responded in a nurturing voice. He patiently listened and explained each question to me. He left the room, and I continued with the test.

The tears were welling up again. The test was taking me so long I felt really stupid. It was time for a break, so I went to the bathroom and washed my face, then I went outside and there was Jack, sitting on the car. It was so wonderful to see him!

"It's been an hour and a half. How much longer do you think you'll be?"

"I don't know. I still have pages and pages to go. Before the wreck, I probably would've finished this exam in "like that" I said, snapping my fingers, but my brain doesn't work the same now, so it's taking me forever. Well, I better get back at it." Jack gave me a kiss and I walked back to my little cubicle.

I plugged away at the questions as best as I could. Every time the doctor came in, I would have another list of questions for him. I might have driven him a little crazy. So many questions I just couldn't figure out how to answer. He helped me with my list as much as he could and disappeared again into his office.

It took over three hours to complete the exam. When I was complete, I looked over my answers again while waiting for the doctor. When Dr. James returned, I gave him my papers and asked, "How long do the results take?"

"I grade these by hand, so I should have it done and filed this week. Of course, it has to go through the proper channels, so it could be a month or two before your lawyer receives the results. How are you doing?"

"I'm still afraid they're going to think I'm crazy and lock me up somewhere."

"I assure you that you are not crazy. That is not what this test is for. I do think you would benefit from some therapy."

"Thank you," I said as we shook hands. "You're probably right."

I went to wash my face one last time, and then went outside. The sun felt warm on my face; it was the feel of freedom. I was exhausted, cramping, grumpy, and wanted to get home. I sat in the sun waiting for Jack. I didn't expect him to sit in the parking lot the whole time. It was no more than three minutes when Jack pulled into the parking lot. I'd been crying again and wiped my face so he wouldn't see. I got into the car and said, "Let's go home please, I am exhausted and all that thinking gave me an atrocious bowling ball headache!"

"You have your meds, right?"

"Yes I do, thank you." I reached into my purse and took a couple pills for the pain but the headache kept getting worse. It was time for a hot shower to loosen everything up so I could get up the stairs; then time for ice and a nap. I don't remember how long the headache lasted. It was one of those thinking headaches no one has ever been able to explain. I still think it was from the concussion. I knew there were pinched nerves in my neck and I needed to get to the chiropractor.

I had very little patience as I waited over three months for the psych exam results. After two months I called the lawyers office to see if the results had come in. All I got was a "not yet." After three months had gone by I called the lawyer's office about the results and I was connected to Brad.

"Are the results in?" I asked anxiously.

"Yes, we finally have the exam results so the judge should also have them."

"Would you mail me a copy of the results?"

"It's a bit unusual to send a client their medical records."

"Please mail me the results; it's the only way I have to get a copy."

"Okay, I will have Camille send it out to you."

"Thank you so much! I appreciate it. How soon do you think

the judge will make a decision, now that the report has been completed?"

"We have to wait until we are scheduled on the judge's docket again."

"Thank you. Keep me posted." I said.

"Will do" he said cheerfully. "Try and have a nice day." And the call was over.

Six months later, yes, *six months* had gone by since the report was completed before we finally received word that we were scheduled on the docket. Jack and I met with the lawyer the week before to go over the protocols again. The lawyer had the updated records of my doctors and medications and we were due in court next week. I felt anxious for days after our meeting. Dr. Benson had put me on anti-depressants some months ago. They helped, but during weeks like this, it wasn't enough. It was time for anxiety meds before my heart beat out of my chest. The disability process had been going on for two and a half years. The wreck settlement was already done. It was time for a decision on disability.

The court date finally came and Jack drove us to the Social Security office downtown. I saw my lawyer heading toward us. A man in a suit and a young couple were in the hall. The young man was very excited and I heard him ask the man in the suit, "We're approved? So when will we get the check?" The man in the suit must have been their lawyer and it seemed that they had been cogs in the system too.

I looked at my lawyer and said, "I guess they finally won. Do you think we have a chance?"

"Yes I do, a very good chance. We have a good judge. He does his paperwork."

We went through the security check and then to one of the small offices. I was jittery. The lawyer looked at us and said, "Well, I have some good news for you." His eyes were twinkling. "I'm rarely wrong, but in this instance, I was a little off. Remember last week I told you that you would be testifying again?" I shook my head and tried to stop trembling. "Well, I know this will really upset you, but you will not be testifying today. Your testimony from our last court date stands as your testimony. The judge will address us first. He has all the updated medical information already so I will have nothing to present. Then the judge will address a doctor on the phone, and remember I rarely cross examine doctors. Then he will speak with the vocational specialist. All you have to do is sit there and be quiet."

I looked at Jack and we both grinned. Me? Stay quiet for an hour? That was hard to visualize. Jack and I decided it would be better for him to sit this one out. When he's in the courtroom, I seem to look at him with every question. It was time to practice being a little jackass keeping my yap shut.

My lawyer looked at me one last time and asked, "Are you ready?"

"I'm as ready as I can be." It was my third time down this rabbit hole. Maybe this time I'll get a glimpse of the wizard.

"All right then, all you have to do is sit and say nothing. Jack, have a seat and we'll meet you out here when we're finished."

We walked into the courtroom and I sat across from the judge in front of the microphone again. The lawyer took his seat to my right. The judge opened the proceedings. Then my lawyer asked me a few questions which I answered. He made a few remarks to the court and then the judge continued with the hearing.

The out-of-town doctor was on the phone now and made the comment that I was able to sit and stand. I quickly scratched a note to my lawyer that said "trouble with sit and stand" and pushed it toward him.

He gave me that "lawyer look" that said "no, your job is to be quiet, I have this handled!" I was angry but kept my mouth shut.

The doctor finished his testimony and he and the judge bid each other good day. The judge looked through some notes and some more paperwork and then was looking at his computer. I was doing my best not to burst like a balloon. It's almost impossible for me to stay quiet for an hour. Of course, since the wreck, that has changed a bit. Don't get me wrong, I can still be a chatterbox. Just ask Jack. He has developed the skill of knowing when to let me ramble so I can blow off steam. Most of the time I think it goes in one ear and out the other. He nods his head politely and looks at me like what I am saying is the most important thing in the world. Then I run out of steam and I am calm again.

I had my hands on the desk and was doing my best not to fidget. There was a box of tissues and bottles of water in front of me. I took several tissues and quietly blew my nose several times. After the doctor testified, everyone in the room was looking at paperwork, flipping through notebooks, or clattering on their keyboards for about fifteen minutes. I sang songs in my head but they eventually went to my lips so I stopped that and concentrated on sitting there quietly. At one point, I think I was even sitting on my hands. My objective was to keep my mouth shut.

The judge looked up from his pulpit and began asking hypothetical questions to the vocational expert. After a few rounds of questions the judge looked at the expert and asked, "Hypothetically speaking, could a person with these limitations be able to contribute to the workforce?"

The vocational expert flipped through her notebook a few more times, looked up at the judge, and replied "No your honor."

The judge scribbled a few notes and then addressed the court. "Well, I think today we need to make the ruling," he paused, I stopped breathing, and my lawyer was looking straight at him, ready for the ruling. The judge asked me several questions to which I answered only "Yes your honor," or "No your honor," as I had been advised.

Then he asked if I had any questions. I looked at my lawyer and his eyes were big as golf balls.

"No your honor."

"I realize this has gone on for quite some time and we are doing our best to fix that. I have heard testimony and I have gone over the records and I'm granting your disability benefits back to your first day of eligibility."

Sadly, this process took so long that the insurance settlement had already been completed. Had I been on disability during the insurance settlement battle, it would have been a different ballgame.

My heart was pounding through my chest but I was still able to keep my mouth shut. I didn't know what the next step would be.

My lawyer said "Thank you, Your Honor."

I quietly repeated, "Thank you, Your Honor," and we left the room.

We found Jack who was waiting patiently outside. We huddled and the lawyer quietly said, "We got it!" Jack looked at me and I nodded yes. The lawyer's eyes grew big, and with a smile he looked right at me and said, "I was so afraid you were going to ask a question."

"You told me my job was to be quiet. You have no idea how hard that was."

"Let's get out of here and talk in the hall." We followed him out of the office and down the hall. "You will get information in the mail. It may take a few months before you see a check, but at least you know you're going to get your check. When it arrives, give me a call. Congratulations, we will be talking soon." We all shook hands and he went on to his next client.

Jack and I were both in shock. We waved goodbye to the security guard for the last time as we floated out the door. I was so excited, I thought I would burst. We took the elevator down to the lobby and, this time, enjoyed the walk next door to the hotel to get our parking ticket stamped. We were ecstatic. Two and a half years of this and now it's over. There would be a check and I could start paying some bills.

Two months went by and a professional looking envelope came in the mail. It was a real check, my eyes watered and I put my hand over my mouth to stifle a squeal.

"Jack, look what came in the mail today." I showed him the envelope and the check. It also came with a letter that explained how the amount was arrived at. The lawyer had already been paid his legal fee out of my check and I was responsible for paying his expenses, which I was happy to pay. I called their office to say thank you and to make sure we were square. The medical circus and the legal trauma drama were paid off in full. No more loopholes!

A feeling of freedom passed through me and I think I even felt joy again. It was the most amazing day. I kept the check for several days while we figured out the best way to use it. We even talked to our financial advisors. We all agreed a little stash would be smart. The rest would be split up to pay down credit cards, the ones with the highest interest rates first, of course. The little stash made me feel more secure after all those years of not being able to pay any bills. It wouldn't pay off the house, but it would tide us over for a few months.

The long journey to receive disability benefits had taken over two and a half years. I was exhausted and exhilarated at the same time. The judge said I would be reevaluated in about three years. At last, no more paperwork or lawyers for a while!

I was able to sit up for almost an hour, taking lots of breaks and I still needed to lie down in the afternoon. When my head turns into a bowling ball, it's time to rest my neck and I still use ice quite frequently.

We deposited the check. It was such a feeling of security to be able to pay the bills. We relaxed that night, still in awe the whole experience had come to an end. With all the excitement, my body started cramping. I am a joyful one and it makes me sad that, when I get really happy or excited, my neck constricts and a nasty headache starts.

In my case, because the whole disability process took so long, I was already eligible and automatically placed on Medicare. I was hoping to learn all that a few years down the road but here I am and grateful to be alive!

Medicare? That's a different book entirely!!

"Just because the past didn't turn out like you wanted it to, doesn't mean your future can't be better than you've ever imagined."

~ Author Unknown

Chapter 33

I Survived! It's Great to Be Alive!

I had endured it all: the wreck, the doctors, the tests, the lawyers and loopholes, the insurance companies, and the disability process. Although I have never regained my strength or endurance, I still believe the human body can heal itself. Just because I haven't found all the right answers doesn't mean it can't be done! Medicine improves my life with modern chemistry and I strive to keep what I have that works, working. I keep my schedule to one thing every other day and I still need to lie down for two hours during the day to help prevent bowling ball head. I do my best to stay within my limits, but some days I don't and I suffer for it.

Last year, I thought about the upcoming anniversary of the wreck. It would be nine years. When that day rolled around, it never came to mind. The only time I saw the woman who hit me was on the day of the wreck and then she moved out of the country. Perhaps she was an angel who ran into me at that exact moment to save me from a semi-truck heading to an upcoming intersection. Who knows? Perhaps she saved my life. That positive view took me years to develop.

I have a few regrets. The first was being in the wreck at all. The biggest regret is that I didn't take the ambulance. I had no business driving after the wreck, but I didn't know that at the time. Another biggie, we totally spaced out on getting pictures of the car after the wreck. We should have picked up an instant camera and done that right away. There's that hindsight again. Another regret is that I didn't call the insurance company before using a lawyer, but they had been so harsh and I couldn't take anymore grief from them. Sometimes I wonder what might have been had the wreck not happened, but not so much these days. This is my life now. It is what I make it.

The farther I move past the wreck, the faster the layers come off. I keep moving forward slowly. All that stress, combined with all that pain, is debilitating. Now with the insurance settlement sealed and the disability battle signed, I have to believe that every year I will continue to get a little better.

When I saw Dr. Benson after everything was finally done, it was time for a shoulder injection for bursitis and another round of steroids for all the inflammation. I had a new understanding of what Dr. Benson meant years ago when he said, if I wasn't depressed, I was in denial. I had started taking another anxiety pill and an anti-depressant. I also agreed to work with a psychiatrist that practiced Cognitive Behavioral Therapy to help me with the PTSD and PTAD. Soon after, Dr. Benson set me up with a Transcutaneous Electrical Nerve Stimulation unit, usually referred to as a TENS unit. It actually helps my shoulders and lower back. The unit uses electrical current to stimulate nerves to block the pain signals.

The psychiatrist did help me with my fear of driving. The Cognitive Behavioral Therapy felt like I was basically telling him my story over and over again every week through the tears. With each session, more details would come up. One week my homework was to drive every day. I didn't like it, but I did it. I knew I had to, if I was going to get my life back. Every visit he would have me tell him my story again and again. After a few months, I told the story with no reaction at all.

"How did that feel?" he asked.

"I am tired of telling the stupid story."

He smiled. Goal accomplished!

The biggest homework challenge was to drive along the same route I had taken the day of the accident. I drove through the wreck site, then to the first police station, and then the second. I didn't remember where the first station was, driving by instinct, I found it the first time. Driving back through town, heading toward the other police station, was bizarre. I was fine driving through the wreck site and travelling about a mile to the highway, but then I drove under the bridge and had no recollection of the rest of the drive. It was surreal! That drive gave me a new feeling of freedom and independence.

I saw this psychiatrist for several months before I was released. When I started back-stepping and hit more hurdles, I called for an appointment, but he was no longer there and had left no forwarding information.

So I called Dr. Donna, the psychologist I worked with decades ago when I was dealing with severe illness. I didn't see any reason to look for someone else. She knew me and I felt very safe with her. She was great. She even remembered me from all those years ago.

For my first few appointments, I came through town on the highway and then onto a busy three-lane main road to get there. There were too many drivers and too many chances to get hit. I told her how hard it was to get to her office. She said it was time to find a different route. She didn't want me worn out from traffic getting to my appointments, especially when driving was one of the main reasons I was seeing her.

As time went on, she jogged my memory and reminded me I have some addictive personality traits. She asked how I was doing with my spending. I realized it was like the last time I worked with her. I was spending money that I didn't have, just to feel alive. I was crying by the time I admitted there were months I spent two grand on stuff, just stuff. She helped me reframe how I looked at myself and money and how unfair it was to Jack that I was getting us in debt. I felt so guilty. I never thought of my online sprees as spending because no cash was involved. I think that's true for many of us who suffer from addictive spending, or maybe it's addiction to debt.

I am glad to say I am attacking that monkey again. I transferred the high balances to zero percent credit card accounts and I am paying off the debt. I spent it, I am taking the responsibility, and I am paying it off. It's time to live in the real world again and she's helping me do that. I remember when I told her I was broken. She rephrased and said, "How about if we use the word damaged?"

"Okay, that doesn't sound so bad I guess. Then there's the brain damage. A friend told me I didn't still have the concussion, I just had the damage that was left."

"And she is right, the concussion is long gone. There may be damage up there, but you are able to function, right?"

"I'm not smart enough to go back to computer work and my body still won't hold up for a whole day."

"But you can get out and do things, you're not stuck somewhere in a coma."

"True." I said.

"So start putting your focus on what you can do without hurting yourself."

"I have been doing some photography. I like to take nature pics. I have a good camera and I promised myself I will not be getting one with all the different lenses; it's too much weight."

"Good. I'd love to see some of your pictures." When I brought some in, she loved them.

I still see her every few weeks. She helps me stay grounded in reality and to keep going. We evaluate and reframe things that come up like the PTSD triggers. She tells me the chances of having another wreck like this one are miniscule. I hear her, but it doesn't help much. I am glad I am seeing her; she helps me more than I can say.

I still see Dr. Benson every two to three months. If I have a flair-up, I call and get in sooner. Flair-ups are so wicked! Everything hurts! Bursitis is a bitch! Sometimes it's injections, sometimes steroids, and sometimes a few weeks of physical therapy. The hard part is to stop doing what causes the flare-ups. Many times it's still difficult to know what caused them because the pain may not show up for hours. No one has figured out that delayed pain thing out yet. My best guess is fractured fascia and connective tissue issues.

I have arthritis in my neck and back, spinal stenosis, bulging discs affecting the nerves in my neck and arms and my lower back, degenerative disc disease, and I still have bursitis flair-ups. But all in all I am glad to be alive! I am glad to be loved!

Shifting the focus to good things, I believe every experience has a gift. Sometimes the gifts are difficult to identify, but they are there. Time can heal wounds if used wisely. A huge gift was discovering Atlas Orthogonal chiropractic and two doctors that are "car wreckologists." Another gift, an old-school orthopedic who knows how to fix me up when my bursitis is burning and my nervous system is inflamed; he's a "car wreckologist" too. After all the legal stuff was done, I found a new MD; one that doesn't stress me out or give me an anxiety attack. Jack even likes him.

The wreck had taken my vitality and love of color away. The whiplash took away many of my vocal abilities. Things have been changing in the last year. Recently I found the most gorgeous tie-dye shirt I had seen in ages. It is bright and brilliant and I had to buy it. My love of color is slowly, finally coming back. I can even sing in the shower now without getting a headache, if I don't push too hard. I'm not good enough for a garage band yet, but I can sing again. During my last visit with Mom she remarked she heard me singing around the house a bit more. I hadn't even noticed.

I embrace the phrase "Patience Little Jackass" better than I used to, although that doesn't stop me from getting impatient. What I used to do in an hour now takes days. What I used to do in days now takes weeks. I still have times when, if I look up too far, my head gets stuck and I have to grab a chunk of hair at the top of my head and literally pull my head back over. When I look down for too long, my head gets stuck in that position and I have to make a fist to cradle my chin and then push my head back up slowly.

I still miss things like singing out loud and bopping my head to music, reading with great comprehension and retention, and shaking my head when I get out of the shower. I miss looking up to the stars or looking down to read a book without pain. I'd like to play my guitar again and look down at the frets and strings without pain.

Then there are things I won't ever do again, like be a systems analyst, ride a roller coaster, go roller skating, drive cross country, or cook a huge Thanksgiving dinner. I've tried. These have become memories of the past; at first bittersweet, but now they are sweet memories.

I still have my limbs and my faculties, even if they don't work the way they used to, at least they work! It costs more to maintain my body these days, but we get by.

Jack and I are doing well, still in love after all the years and tears. I bestow my best husband award upon him, again and again, for loving me and always believing in me. It's a feeling beyond definition.

So, thank you to the doctors and the lawyers and the paralegals that helped me through the madness!

I'm especially grateful for all those people who still love me and didn't give up on me through my years of torment....

I made it through years of tears. I made it through the dark times, the up times, the down times, and the in-between times. I made it through...and so can YOU!

It has now been over ten years since the wreck. Things DO get better! Be gentle with yourself; love yourself and all that you have! Start with baby steps and go at your own speed. There are no time limits. It takes as long as it takes. When you are ready, start using your time wisely. Allow yourself to grieve, help yourself to heal, laugh, and most importantly, feel joy again! Believe things will work out.

Find positive things about your life. Find the gifts! Write them on sticky notes and place them around the house. If you see no positives in the moment, start with "I am alive" or "I have a friend" or "I have food." Spark the gratitude inside you for all that you do have! Maybe even work up to "I love myself just the way I am." If you walked for ten minutes and the goal was six minutes, how about "I walked ten minutes!" Celebrate! Celebrate every step forward, no matter how small. Put a check in the improvement column!

Check local hospitals, community centers, and Hospice for classes and support groups. Keep doing your physical therapy exercises. With your doctor's permission, check your neighborhood community centers and local gyms; join one and use it. They may have services available that you can't do at home, like warm pool classes, or maybe a machine you used in PT. When checking out a new gym, make certain it has everything YOU need, or there is no point in joining. If that's not in the budget, ask your doctor about using a DVD for your level to work out with at home; maybe just start with a stretching program.

Love yourself! You can do this! You can!

I hope this book has given you enlightenment and education.

I hope you are inspired to move forward with courage and optimism.

You can only do what you can do, so do what you can with what you have.

Be gentle with yourself. Be grateful you are here!

Each Day Brings a New Beginning, a New Opportunity…

A New Day of Life…Cherish It!

"Surround yourself with
the dreamers and the doers,
the believers and the thinkers,
but most of all,
surround yourself with those
who see the greatness within you,
even when you don't see it yourself."

~ Edmund S. Lee

About the Author

Wendy Teague is an author, speaker, energy practitioner and consultant. For over 20 years Wendy has worked with vibrational, frequency, and resonance healing for individuals, groups, and long distance healing. She loves helping people demystify energy work and learn to self-heal the multiple layers of their being. She has developed programs working specifically to clear the compound traumas of people's lives, including fear, emotional pain, and other issues that keep them stuck in the past.

Wendy is the owner and CEO of Essential Energetics, located in Independence, Missouri. She has introduced thousands of people and animals to the culture and benefits of energy healing through her lectures, classes, and individual and group sessions. She has been a Certified Resonance Repatterning® Practitioner since 1997 and received her Certification in the Yuen Method® in 2004. Wendy also has a strong background in sound healing, essential oils, and crystal healing.

Before shifting into full-time energy practice in 1997, Wendy had a successful 20-year career in the corporate arena as a computer systems analyst.

As a survivor and thriver of multiple devastating traumas, both physical and emotional, Wendy has experienced what it's like to live in pain and suffering from illness, surgery, and injury... and how the energetic impact can drain your passion for life.

Wendy experienced the exhilaration of discovering caring professionals combined with self-healing options that restored her balance and function, and helped her reconnect to her inner potential and joy.

After encountering an abrasive medical system and an impersonal insurance system, Wendy was driven with passion to reclaim her power by sharing her experience with others and give them support and guidance in navigating the obstacle course that begins after a life-changing event occurs. Her book "After the Wreck" addresses core challenges faced by both the injured and their caregivers. Since completing her book Wendy has become an in demand guest on radio, television, and online. To work with Wendy personally, book her for your show, or have her speak at your event, go to www.AfterTheWreck.com.

Resources and Suggestions

These books were used in courses I attended and really helped me along my journey. No special classes needed as they are both readily available to the public.

Living a Healthy Life with Chronic Conditions Self-Management of Heart Disease, Arthritis, Diabetes, Asthma, Bronchitis, Emphysema and others Third Edition, by Kate Lorig, RN, DrPH, Halstead Holman, MD, David Sobel, MD, Diana Laurent, MPH, Virginia González, MPH, and Marian Minor, RPT, PhD Contributer Peg Harrison, MA, MSW, LCSW Copyright © 2006 Bull Publishing Company, Boulder, CO

The Grief Recovery Handbook: The Action Program for Moving Beyond Death, Divorce, and Other Losses including Health, Career, and Faith, 20th Anniversary Expanded Edition, by John W. James and Russell Friedman Copyright © 2009 by John W. James and Russell Friedman, Harper-Collins Publishers, New York

Check local listings in your community for Hospice, hospitals and community centers. They may have classes and / or support groups you may feel will help you. Trust your instincts.

Glossary

Acute — a fast onset with a short healing time. It has a beginning and an end. Like a paper cut, you suddenly have it and in a few days it is healed.

Anxiety — fear, apprehension and worry occurring without a present threat.

Anxiety Disorder — recurring anxiety, unable to focus, symptoms include excessive worry and apprehension. Fear of the future and the unknown. The uncertainty may be from actual or perceived events. Anxiety may affect both the physical and psychological health. Continuous anxiety may become debilitating.

Atlas Orthogonal Chiropractic (AO) — a discipline of chiropractic developed by Dr. Roy W. Sweat, D.C. that focuses on the relationship between the skull and the top cervical vertebra (the atlas), and then addresses the full spine. When the atlas is adjusted into proper position, adjustment of the rest of the spine is easier to align with gentle techniques.

Chakra — energy centers in the human body. Their name derives from the Sanskrit word for "wheel", but in yogic context a better translation is "vortex." The best known chakras are the seven centers that run up the center of the body. Different teachings present different numbers of chakras.

Chi — the vital energy of the body. There are many names in many cultures used for this such as Life Force, Qi, and Mana.

Chi Gong — also known as Qigong or Chi Kung, a practice that aligns breath with movement and awareness. It is used for exercise, healing and meditation.

Chronic — goes on and on and on…A chronic condition is persistent with long lasting effects.

Cognitive Behavioral Therapy (CBT) — a technique used in psychotherapy to address dysfunctional emotions, behaviors, and cognitive processes. Treatment focuses on the specific problems of the individual. The process is goal oriented to help the patient find acceptable strategies that will help address the problems.

CranioSacral Therapy (CST) — developed by John Upledger, D.O. is a hands-on approach to health care that utilizes a light touch on various key areas of the body to relieve restrictions in the dural membrane that surrounds and protects the spinal cord. Relieving these restrictions promotes the healthy flow of cerebrospinal fluid, which in turn promotes health and healing to all areas of the physical body.

Electroencephalography (EEG) — charts brain waves by recording electrical activity using multiple electrodes placed on the scalp.

Electromyography (EMG) — checks neural pathway connections. Simple electrodes are placed on opposite ends of the muscle. A signal is sent between the electrodes. If the signal is moving through the muscle, that electrical activity will cause the muscle to jump around, you have no control over it. I refer to this one as the "frog test."

Essential Oils — just as we have blood that runs life force through our veins, so have plants. Oil is collected from the plant using various methods. The use of essential oils goes back to the bible and beyond. The skin absorbs the oil through the pores which are much larger than the molecular structures of the oil.

Evaluation—assessment, testing, looking at how the body moves.

Fascia—a sheet or band of connective tissue that surrounds muscle, bones, nerves, and organs. Fascia is everywhere in the human body.

Hydrotherapy—a form of medicine that uses water for therapy. It is used primarily in occupational therapy and physical therapy for pain relief. Water encompasses many possibilities for therapy, such as temperature, pressure, whirlpool baths, baths with water jets, and mineral baths. It can stimulate circulation and help alleviate symptoms. Examples of home care with hydrotherapy include hot showers, cool baths, and whirlpool tubs.

Hypnosis—a trance-like, induced state of calm relaxation where deeper parts of the mind are more accessible. You are more open to suggestion, but you don't lose control over your behavior.

Independent Medical Exam or Examiner (I.M.E.)—when a doctor, with no previous relationship with the patient, examines the individual and all their medical records. I.M.E.s are used to determine cause and extent of injuries, identify any permanent damage, and to ascertain if the individual has reached the maximum benefit from medical treatment. The examiner is an advocate for the record, there is no patient doctor relationship.

Interrogatories—a formal legal document with a set of questions to be answered in writing. Fancy legal term for answer these questions.

Massage—there are many types of massage. The most commonly known is Swedish massage. Some massage is done with a light touch, some medium, while others go very deep into the muscles. Massage promotes good circulation and helps with lymphatic drainage. Massage can help to free it up stuck muscles and fascia.

Mediation — a process used before going to trial, sometimes ordered by a judge, the purpose is to reach a settlement between the parties without a trial

Meridians — rivers of energy that flow throughout your body. Most commonly associated with Acupuncture from traditional Chinese medicine.

Magnetic Resonance Imaging (MRI) — a medical imaging technique used to see the detailed internal structures of the body. MRIs have much more detail than an X-ray.

Myofascial Release (MFR) — a soft tissue therapy used to treat pain and help with restricted motion. The practitioner uses palpation and the body's feedback to achieve optimal results. Myofascial Release helps relax contracted muscles which increases circulation and lymphatic drainage.

Neurology — a medical specialty that deals with disorders of the brain and the central and peripheral nervous systems.

Neuropsychology — the study of brain function and structure relating to specific psychological process and behaviors. The goal is to study, understand and treat behaviors directly related to brain function. To some this is considered an experimental field of psychology.

Pain Management — a billion-dollar industry that "manages" pain symptoms.

Panic — sudden, unreasoning fear! The sudden perception of fear tends to prevent reason and logic and activates a person's fight-flight response. Panic can occur whether a threat is real or perceived filling a person with overwhelming anxiety or frantic behavior.

Past Life Regression—a technique using hypnosis to recover past memories. Some may seek information from a past life and for others they only regress to a part of this lifetime to identify repressed memories. The regression technique may be applied to many situations in many different ways.

Physical Therapy (PT)—therapy for the physical body. The therapist evaluates the patient and provides a plan of individualized therapy. This may include stretching exercises, working with exercise bands, or different machines. Each exercise is generally focused on a specific muscle group.

Post-Traumatic Stress Disorder (PTSD)—a severe condition that may develop after one or more serious or perceived traumas. Although each case is different, symptoms generally last more than a month and may include recurring flashbacks, avoiding the past, numbing out with drugs or alcohol, high anxiety levels and nightmares. Most people who experience trauma do not develop PTSD.

Qi—the vital energy of the body. There are many names in many cultures used for this such as Life force and Chi, and Mana. Qi translates to natural energy, life force or energy flow. Similar concepts are found in many cultures.

Reiki—developed by Japanese Buddhist MikaoUsui in 1922. Originally a spiritual practice, it has been adapted by various traditions. Reiki is a healing discipline that can be practiced hands on or with no touch, and also by long distance.

Regression Therapy—takes you back in time. Using your mind you can control your thoughts and go backwards to a specific place and time. This technique is much easier when you have someone guiding you through your regression.

Resonance Repatterning® (formerly known as Holographic Repatterning®)— developed by Chloe Faith Wordsworth. This extraordinary process can help identify and clear the unconscious energetic patterns underlying any issue or problem you may be experiencing. Resonance Repatterning helps you align with what you do want so manifesting becomes an easier and more natural process.

Sacroiliac (SI) Joints—the joints in the pelvis between the sacrum and the ilium of the pelvis, joined by ligaments, connecting the pelvis to the spine. Ideally, the right and left SI joints move together as one unit.

Sleep Hygiene—keeping a consistent schedule to help with the body's sleep cycle such as getting up at the same time daily as well as going to bed at the same time daily. A good sleep is very important for living and for healing.

Transcutaneous Electrical Nerve Stimulation (TENS) **Unit**—a non-invasive, low-risk option intended to reduce pain. The unit uses electrical current to stimulate nerves and treat pain through electrodes attached to the skin.

White Coat Syndrome—also called "white coat hypertension" is a significant fear or anxiety around doctors. Patients tend to have elevated blood pressure in the clinical setting but nowhere else. The theory is the patient suffers anxiety during a doctor visit, causing their blood pressure to be higher.

Yuen Method® (YM)—developed by Dr. Kam Yuen. This energetic method addresses the body's supercomputer, working directly with the body's software, firmware, and operating system to create energetic change.

www.ingramcontent.com/pod-product-compliance
Lightning Source LLC
Chambersburg PA
CBHW060248100426
42742CB00011B/1681